Joining the Resistance

Carol Gilligan

—————

JOINING THE RESISTANCE

polity

First published in 2011 by Polity Press

Polity Press
65 Bridge Street
Cambridge CB2 1UR, UK

Polity Press
350 Main Street
Malden, MA 02148, USA

ISBN-13: 978-0-7456-5169-9

A catalogue record for this book is available from the British Library.

Typeset in 11 on 14 pt Sabon
by Servis Filmsetting Ltd, Stockport, Cheshire
Printed and bound in the US by Edwards Brothers Inc.

The publisher has used its best endeavors to ensure that the URLs for external websites referred to in this book are correct and active at the time of going to press. However, the publisher has no responsibility for the websites and can make no guarantee that a site will remain live or that the content is or will remain appropriate.

Every effort has been made to trace all copyright holders, but if any have been inadvertently overlooked the publisher will be pleased to include any necessary credits in any subsequent reprint or edition.

For further information on Polity, visit our website: www.politybooks.com

This book is for Diana de Vegh

. . . Isn't the
    honesty
of things where they
    resist,
where only the wind
    can bend them

back, the real weather . . .

                    Jorie Graham

Contents

Introduction

In the summer when I was two-and-a-half, my mother, a forward-looking woman interested in the latest developments and invested in raising her child, took me to Clara Thompson's institute at Vassar College designed to impart psychoanalytic wisdom to the parents of young children. Like many such experiments, it was conceived with the best of intentions: the children would attend nursery school while the parents learned about child development. Though set in the midst of American society, it was organized like a kibbutz: the children would live in one building or dormitory while the parents lived in another. It was an arrangement my two-year-old self could not imagine, despite the careful preparation. I loved the nursery school and my teacher whose name I remember to this day, but when it came to bedtime, I wanted my mother, not some *metapelet*, to put me to sleep. And so, at a very young age, I discovered the power of voice to bring about change. Like Joshua with his trumpet at Jericho, I found that by crying loud enough and long enough walls *can* come

1

tumbling down. The rules gave way and my mother was summoned. An exception was granted: she could put me to bed and sing me to sleep. I never learned what Clara Thompson thought of this breach in practice and can only imagine what was said about me to justify this irregularity, but my mother, God bless her, always cherished this display of spirit on my part, whatever embarrassment it may have caused her, and it's possible that the other children also enjoyed her singing.

Years later, I found an ethical rationale for what at two was a protest against resignation. It was the late 1960s, I had completed my Ph.D. in psychology, and being the mother of three young children, I was looking for part-time work. At a party given by a friend, I was introduced to Lawrence Kohlberg. His theory of moral development captured the passion for justice that had inspired me along with many members of my generation to take action on behalf of civil rights and to protest what we saw as an unjust war. When he offered me a job as a research assistant, I accepted and thus became involved in the lively discussions provoked by his claim, following Socrates, that virtue is one and its name is justice. Moral development follows a single path, leading beyond self-interest and societal conventions to a principled understanding of justice as fairness. It was a theory that captured the spirit of the time, providing a justification for civil disobedience.

For a long time, I did not see the connection between my early experience at Vassar and the questions about voice and resistance that have inspired my research. It explains my optimism about the possibility of having an effect, even against considerable odds. Yet what strikes me more particularly is that my resistance to losing a ground of relationship I had taken for granted was a resistance I would see again in four- and five-year-old boys and in adolescent girls. And even at these later ages, when the issue was not wanting their mother, it brought them up against institutional structures that seemed firmly entrenched.

Over the past forty years, a confluence of evidence in the human sciences, coming from developmental psychology and sociology, neurobiology and evolutionary anthropology, has shown that we are, by nature, responsive, relational beings, born with a voice and into relationship, hard-wired for empathy and cooperation, and that our capacity for mutual understanding was—and may well be—key to our survival as a species. When I say this on a panel in the fall of 2010, I am contradicted by my two co-panelists, both distinguished academics—told in no uncertain terms that by nature we are aggressive and competitive, driven by evolution to the pursuit of self-interest. What accounts for this disparity?

In her artist's statement for her exhibition "Proud Flesh," the photographer Sally Mann identifies herself as "a woman who looks." Photographing her husband of forty years, "let[ting] the sunshine fall voluptuously on a still beautiful form," the two of them "still in love, still at work," she is aware of the risk she is taking:

> Within traditional narratives, women who look, especially women who look unflinchingly at men, have been punished: Take poor Psyche, punished for all time for daring to lift the lantern to finally see her lover ... The

act of looking appraisingly at a man, making eye contact on the street, asking to photograph him, studying his body, has always been a brazen venture for a woman, though for a man these acts are commonplace, even expected.

I remember standing in the Gagosian gallery on Madison Avenue on a rainy Thursday afternoon, the luminosity of the photographs like light from a distant star. I had never seen a man photographed in this way before, with an eye so loving, so insistent on seeing. Alone in the quiet gallery, I realized that Mann had broken a taboo.

It's true that the mythical Psyche was punished for breaking Eros's injunction against her seeing him or speaking about their love. When she lifted the lantern, she was planning to kill him, having been told by her sisters that he was a monster, intent on devouring her and their child. What stilled her hand was his beauty, and also his humanness, his vulnerability. The stories about him turned out not to be true. What she saw was what she had known about him in darkness and silence: he was a tender and responsive man. And although Eros does carry out his threat to leave her if she tries to see him, and Psyche is subjected to all manner of torments and trials, the story has a happy ending. Joined as equals in a just and everlasting marriage, Psyche and Eros become the parents of a daughter named Pleasure. It's easy to forget this ending, because the path leading to happiness seems so improbable.

Like Mann, I have lived in a long marriage, still in love and still at work. My husband and I have raised three sons. My mother loved men and I grew up loving two fathers, my father and also his father who lived with us through most of my childhood. When I went back to Harvard after graduate school to teach part-time, I gravitated to Erik Erikson and Lawrence Kohlberg whom I recognized as intelligent and sensitive men, with a playful side like my grandfather and an ethical sensibility like my father. Knowing them personally, I could see the roots of their work in their lives. Erik had named himself Erikson after discovering that he had grown up not knowing that he was the son of a Danish man; Kohlberg had been caught as a child in the moral dilemma precipitated by his parents' divorce: should his mother give up custody of him in order to enable him to secure his inheritance from his wealthy father? Both men became fathers to me in the sense of showing me a way into psychology that engaged my interests, and by their example encouraged me to pursue my own questions. I did not anticipate that by following in their footsteps (as they had followed Freud and Piaget), I would find myself in forbidden territory. It was one thing to bring men's lives into history and generalize from men's experience. To do so with women broke a silence.

To paraphrase Mann, I am a woman who listens. My research began with questions about voice: Who is speaking, and to whom? In what body? Telling what stories about relationships? In what societal and cultural frameworks? My ear had been caught by two things: a silence among men, and an absence of resonance when women said what they were really thinking and feeling. By inquiring into what men were not saying and by providing some resonance for women, I heard a voice that had been held in silence. It was like shifting the frequency and suddenly hearing a station that had been jammed. I wrote *In a Different Voice* to make sense of a dissonance between women's voices and the voice of prevailing psychological theories. In the process, I realized the extent to which we, meaning both men and women, had been telling false stories about ourselves.

In the tale of "The Emperor's New Clothes," it is a child who says that the emperor is naked. In Hawthorne's novel, *The Scarlet Letter*, seven-year-old Pearl sees what the Goodwives and Puritans cannot discern: the connection between her mother and the minister. In my research, it was an eleven-year-old girl who responded to my saying "this interview is just between you and me" by adding "and your tape recorder." When I went on to explain that the tape would only be listened to by other members of the research group, she asked, "Then why don't they just all come into the room?" Disruptive questions. I needed her to take what I said at face value so I could get on with my work, and in fact, she agreed to my terms, choosing a name she wanted us to use in place of her own. But from then on, she sounded depressed. The price of staying in relationship with me was to not say what she was seeing and to act as if what I had said made sense.

I couldn't listen to children and go on working in the same way. What stopped me was the realization that I was becoming complicit in overcoming their resistance to not saying what they saw or knowing what they knew. At Halloween, in a fifth-grade classroom, I watched the girls look up at the ceiling as their teacher read story after story in which a woman was strangled or otherwise mangled. They loved their teacher, who

Introduction

was a woman; they knew she didn't want them to notice this.

The resistance that gripped my attention was a resistance to dissociation. In coming of age, the girls were aware of but also resisting pressures to disengage themselves from their honest voices. Exploring their resistance, I saw how it challenged an initiation that was both culturally sanctioned and socially enforced. In many ways, it was adaptive if not essential to praise the emperor's new clothes and not see that the minister who professed to love the truth, was, in his own words, "living a lie"—as the minister says in Hawthorne's novel.

I had not remembered that the word "patriarchy" appears repeatedly in *The Scarlet Letter*. I had read the novel as a tragic love story and a cautionary tale about the wages of sin. But there it was, right on the page: "patriarchal privilege," "patriarchal deacon" (pp. 199, 200), along with the confession:

> I used to watch and study this patriarchal personage [the Father of the Custom-House] with, I think, livelier curiosity than any other form of humanity there presented to my notice. He was, in truth, a rare phenomenon; so perfect in one point of view; so shallow, so delusive, so impalpable, such an absolute nonentity, in every other. (p. 16)

I had associated patriarchy with anthropology and the study of ancient tribes, and also with a feminism that saw men as monsters. Yet in writing a play inspired by *The Scarlet Letter*, and turning the play into a libretto for an opera called "Pearl," my son Jonathan and I were repeatedly struck by the depth of Hawthorne's insights into what is not usually thought of as the American dilemma: the tension between the radical Protestant vision of an unmediated relationship with God (who can be worshipped by anyone, anywhere—at home, in the forest, as well as in church) and the continuation of an all-male clerical hierarchy; between the vision of a democratic society, a shining city on the hill, and the continuation of patriarchal power and privilege. In an aria for the opera, we ask: "If God is love, how can love be sin?"

I had taken Shakespeare & Company's month-long actor-training workshop to learn from Tina Packer and Kristin Linklater what theater people know about voice. I began to experience how voice lives in the body, how it is connected to breath and the physical world of sound and vibration, as well as to language and culture. I discovered how dissociation can be enacted through the body, how precisely it can come to pass that, as sixteen-year-old Tanya reflects, "the voice that stands up for what I believe in is buried deep inside me." Buried, not lost. Having seen girls resist self-silencing and noting the conflicts that followed, within themselves and in the adults around them, I realized that in order to understand what I was seeing, I had to ask: resistance to what?

My work branched out in two directions. To explore dissociation or dissociative processes, to understand how it is that we can separate ourselves from parts of ourselves and come not to know what we know, I entered psychoanalysis and the more associative world of the arts where emotion is not walled off from thought. I began to focus more on the physical voice, hearing it as an instrument of expression as well as a concept or metaphor for the self. I continued to work in the theater, co-directing an all-women Shakespeare company and writing a play as well as a novel. An invitation to join the Social and Political Sciences faculty at the University of Cambridge and subsequently to teach in the law school at NYU provided opportunities to explore the politics as well as the psychology of resistance and to plant my study of resistance more firmly in a social and political landscape.

I had come full circle, joining my interest in psychology with an ongoing commitment to the arts and to political activism, but, the times were a changing. My work became more radical and more incendiary. In the 1990s, for the first time since suffrage, women's votes elected the president, and in the contested presidential election of 2000, the largest divergence between men's and women's votes was recorded (with more men voting for Bush and more women for Gore). In the U.S. healthcare debates, an ethic of care was countered by death threats; the word "patriarchy" was dismissed as archaic even as its manifestations became more apparent in the rise of religious fundamentalism and the attacks on Hillary Clinton; and the death of feminism was repeatedly proclaimed.

The inspiration for this book crystallized in 2009, prompted by three events: the French publisher Flammarion revised their original translation of *In a Different Voice* and published a new edition, and Fushoka, the Japanese publisher, decided to re-translate the book; a cover story in *The New Yorker* asked "Why is feminism still so divisive?"; and, in a realization of what in the '60s had simply been a dream, Barack Obama was inaugurated as president of the United States.

The actual writing began on a Saturday in May. I was standing on the *Rue Monge*, having come to Paris to celebrate the publication of the revised French translation. My husband and I were spending the month in a rented flat, and I had gone for a walk to allay my anxiety about speaking at the public seminar organized by the scholars who had called for the revision and sponsored by the formidable *École des hautes études en sciences sociales*. Images came flooding back of previous presentations to the academy: of the time shortly after *In a Different Voice* was published, when I was invited to face my critics at the Society for Research in Child Development. The all-women panel was held in the hotel ballroom and introduced by Eleanor Maccoby, a distinguished scholar and expert on sex differences. She began her remarks by quoting a colleague, "male of course," she said, who had stopped her to say: "See you at the shoot-out at the OK Corral." She then went on to override her linking of shoot-outs with men by stating that there was no evidence of psychological sex differences, a position she would later gracefully retract. I remembered my gratitude at the time to Catherine Snow, the last of the women to speak on the panel and a scholar of language development, who pointed out that to establish the existence of a different voice, all I needed was a single example. Gender was a red herring, but it was also a powerful lens.

Introduction

Standing on the Paris street, a cacophony of voices rang in my ears, some encouraging, others grating. My research findings had been described as ground breaking but also, at the height of the 2000 Gore vs. Bush campaign, as providing the ground for a "war against boys" (on the assumption that my conclusions would lead to resources being diverted away from boys and toward girls). I found that my responses did little to dispel such attacks.

I had met Sandra Laugier and Patricia Papperman, the moral philosopher and the sociologist who organized the seminar, in a café across from the Luxembourg Gardens. We had talked about care ethics and care work, the subjects of their research. They did not shy away from the politics of gender or the word "feminist." As Sandra had written, "theories of care, like many radical feminist theories, suffer from misrecognition ... because contrary to general 'gender' approaches, a veritable ethics of care cannot exist without social transformation."

And perhaps it was finding this resonance for my deepest intention, coupled with the joy of being in Paris, that spurred my desire to re-enter a conversation that had become mired in the "justice vs. care debate." A fleeting wish that my new French colleagues would now speak on my behalf gave way to what in that moment on the street in Paris felt like a revelation: who better than I to speak to the misunderstandings and mistranslations of my work. I returned to the flat with fresh energy and a clear intention: I would address the misconceptions and give voice to my present concerns about the need for an ethic of care, the situation of women and men, and a potential for social transformation that lay in our midst.

The writing I began in Paris continued over the ensuing year. Circling back over the past, I came to my current take on the major themes of my work. Certain themes and topics recur as I approach them from different angles or see them in a new light as part of a larger pattern. For example, I will return repeatedly to the research with girls because that was the opening—the way into a mystery in the lives of not only girls and women but also boys and men. The voices of girls had struck a resonant chord, the changes observed could readily be seen, but the implications deepened when subsequent research revealed similar patterns in boys' development, and findings in evolutionary anthropology and neurobiology also challenged longstanding assumptions about human nature. What had seemed an aberration or particular to girls now appeared as a manifestation of a more general resistance to losing the grounds of our humanity.

My title, *Joining the Resistance*, comes from the Tanner Lecture on Human Values that I gave at the University of Michigan in 1990. There, for the first time, I spoke publicly about the psychology and politics of resistance. I have expanded the lecture and given it a new title, including it here (Chapter 4) to recall the voices of the girls and women who first led me to see that the requisites for love and for citizenship in a democratic society are one and the same. Both voice and the desire to live in relationships inhere in our human nature, along with the capacity to resist false authority.

The optimism I took from my summer at Vassar

about the possibility of having an effect (even against considerable odds) and the insight that a veritable ethics of care "cannot exist without social transformation" came together in the recognition that the seeds for such transformation lie within ourselves.

1 Looking Back to Look Forward: Revisiting *In a Different Voice*

In the course of editing *In a Different Voice*, in the days before computers, Harvard University Press sent out the manuscript to be re-typed. Some weeks later, I went to pick it up. The typist, a young woman, lived in a brown, three-decker house in a working-class neighborhood of Somerville. I waited while she retrieved the manuscript, which she was so taken with, she explained, that she had given it to her cousin to read. Standing on the porch, I registered my delight in the realization that the appeal of my book was wider than I had imagined.

Some months after the book was published, the sales rep from the Press took me to lunch. As we waited for coffee, he asked the question that was clearly on his mind: Why is this book selling? I thought of the typist and her cousin who lived upstairs. People whose voices were dismissed felt heard.

Looking back now, it is perhaps easier to see that my title, *In a Different Voice*, calls for a new way of speaking, a change in the very terms of the conversation about ourselves and morality, women and men—about the human condition. In the old conversation, our ears were accustomed to hearing "He was an interesting talker; a man who had traveled all over the world and lived in half a dozen countries," and "Well, Susan, this is a fine mess you are in." I had borrowed these sentences from Strunk and White's *The Elements of Style* (where they demonstrate the correct use of semi-colons and commas) to illustrate a point of view so widely assumed that for a long time we did not notice it. Once seen, the point of view shifted. In the newly illustrated 2008, fiftieth anniversary edition of *The Elements of Style*, the interesting talker has become "she" and Susan is pictured as a basset hound.

At the time I wrote *In a Different Voice*, I was aware of a problem in psychology that was in part a problem of method (the selection of boys and men only for studies of human development) and partly a problem of theory (a point of view from which men's lives appeared interesting and women's more or less of a mess). Clearly there was a problem, but in some ways the most interesting thing—at least to a psychologist's eye—was that it had not been seen. Since I was among those who hadn't seen it, despite the fact that I was teaching psychology, I asked: How could this have happened? In one sense, I was discovering the obvious.

Gender proved the tell-tale clue, not by locating the problem in women or men, but by pointing to where all this was coming from. A colleague in anthropology used to say that culture appears in the unspoken. Culture is the way of seeing and speaking that is so much a part of everyday living that it never has to be articulated. Fish don't know they are swimming in water, until they are a fish out of water. It is when culture shifts that we recognize the ocean in which we have been drenched. What we had taken as natural or taken for granted becomes instead one way of seeing and speaking. By the 1970s, I along with many others had come to John Berger's realization: "Never again will a single story be taken as though it's the only one."

In the changing culture of that time, in my early days of teaching, I heard myself respond to a woman's question by saying, "That's a great question, but it's not what we're talking about here." And then found myself wondering, who is this "we" and what are we talking about? Reasonable questions at any time, but at the height of the women's movement, I realized that I had aligned myself with a cultural standpoint from which women's questions, however great, were for the most part beside the point. Writing *In a Different Voice*, I broke this alignment, divorcing myself from ways of speaking that portrayed men as humans and women as different. Recognizing the extent to which I had been swimming along as if it made sense to title a book *The Psychological World of the Teenager: A Study of Normal Adolescent Boys*, as Daniel and Judith Offer had done, or to move seamlessly from *The Seasons of a Man's Life* to *Stages of Adult Development*, as Daniel Levinson had done, again in collaboration with his wife, I realized that neither men nor women were noticing the omission of girls and women, or seeing it as a problem. Psychologists had assumed a culture in which men were the measure of humanity, and autonomy and rationality ("masculine" qualities) were the markers of maturity. It was a culture that counted on women not speaking for themselves.

And here morality came into play. Not in the usual sense of establishing right and wrong, good and bad, but by enforcing women's silence in the name of goodness. The good woman cared for others: she listened to their voices and responded to their needs and concerns. In itself, a good thing to do. But this ethic of feminine goodness was holding in place so-called normal, everyday conversations in which men spoke as if the omission of women was irrelevant or inconsequential and women overlooked or excused the omission of themselves.

Once it is clear that the different voice with its ethic of care resists these divisions, it becomes easier to grasp the reasons for common misunderstandings and mistranslations of my work, to recognize how parts of my original text contributed to these misunderstandings, and also to see how these misinterpretations reflect an assimilation of my work to the very gender norms and values I was contesting. And seeing this focuses the questions I want to raise in revisiting my 1982 book. Given the value of care and caring and the costs of carelessness, why is an ethic of care still embattled? What is the justice vs. care debate about? And what is the relationship of all this to women? Why are women's voices still in the forefront in bringing these matters to our attention?

If anything, an ethic of care is more pressing now than at the time I first wrote about it, almost thirty years ago, and questions of gender are in some respects more difficult to raise and discuss. We live in a world increasingly alert to the reality of interdependence and the costs of isolation; we know that autonomy is an illusion—that

17

people's lives are interconnected. In 1963, the Reverend Martin Luther King Jr. had observed: "We are caught in an inescapable network of mutuality, tied in a single garment of destiny. What affects one directly affects all indirectly." We understand more about trauma, its neurological as well as its psychological effects. In his first address to Congress, President Obama spoke about carelessness—its effects on health, education, the economy, the planet—and the need to replace an ethos of individual gain with an ethic of care and collective responsibility. But during the 2008 presidential campaign, where racist comments were not tolerated, it was still okay for media pundits to say that they instinctively crossed their legs at the mention of Hillary Clinton's name, or to refer to her as a "hellish housewife," witchy, bitchy, a "she-devil." As one Fox News commentator put it, "When Hillary Clinton speaks, men hear 'take out the garbage'." Obama's call to understand and then transcend longstanding and embittered conversations about race was not met with a similar call for a new conversation about gender. Why?

Indeed, why is the ethic of care still embattled? What is the academic debate over care vs. justice about? And what is its association with women and more generally with people's lives? I cannot go further in talking about gender—a word I associated with Latin vocabulary—without speaking about its relation to patriarchy, an order of living based upon gender: where being a man means not being a woman and also being on top. The gender binary and hierarchy are the DNA of patriarchy—the building blocks of a patriarchal order. The word "patriarchy" means a hierarchy or rule of priests in which the *hieros*, the priest, is a *pater*, a father. In a patriarchal family or religion or culture, power and authority descend from a father or fathers, and human qualities designated masculine are privileged over those gendered feminine. By elevating some men over others (separating the men from the boys) and all men over women, patriarchy is an order of domination. But in separating fathers from mothers and daughters and sons, and bifurcating *human* qualities into masculine and feminine, patriarchy also creates rifts in the psyche, dividing everyone from parts of themselves.

In the gendered universe of patriarchy, care is a *feminine ethic*, not a universal one. Caring is what good women do, and the people who care are doing women's work. They are devoted to others, responsive to their needs, attentive to their voices. They are *selfless*.

I entered the conversation about women and morality in the late 1960s, a time in the U.S. that witnessed a convergence of the civil rights movement, the anti-war movement, the movement to stop atmospheric testing of nuclear weapons, the movement to end poverty, the women's movement, and the gay liberation movement. I was teaching at Harvard with Erik Erikson, a psychoanalyst working in the Freudian tradition, and Lawrence Kohlberg, a cognitive-developmental psychologist working in the tradition of Piaget. To all these men—Freud and Erikson, Piaget and Kohlberg—women appeared deficient in development. Women's investment in relationships was considered to be at the expense of a clear sense of self and women's emotional responsiveness was said to compromise their capacity to think rationally and judge objectively. Thus the paradox noted in *In a Different Voice*: the very qualities that distinguished women's moral goodness, their relational sensitivity and empathic concern, marked them as deficient in development.

In the 1970s, these assumptions were called into question. I remember interviewing a woman at that time, asking her to respond to one of the dilemmas used in assessing moral development, and she looked at me and said: "Do you want to know what I think? Or do you want to know what I really think?" Indicating that she had learned to think in a way that differed from how she really thought.

I was interested in identity and moral development, and began to explore people's responses to actual situations of moral conflict and choice, times when the sense of self, the I, comes to the fore in the question "What am I going to do?" and moral language (should, ought, right, wrong, good, bad) comes into play in the questions "What should I do?" or "What is the right or good thing to do?" My study was prompted by an observation I made in teaching a discussion section of Kohlberg's course on moral and political choice. I noticed that the men in my class—some in preppy outfits, cooperative and polite, others long-haired in jeans and Gandhi shirts—although eager to talk about the injustice of the Vietnam War, fell silent when the conversation turned to the ethics of draft resistance. They were aware that if they said what they were really thinking, namely that their thoughts about resisting the draft hinged in part on relationships and feelings, they would sound like women and be scored at a lower stage of moral development. I interviewed these students at the end of their sophomore year, asking about their experiences of moral conflict and choice, and planned to interview them again as seniors when they would be facing the draft—but then President Nixon ended the draft.

This was in 1973, the year the U.S. Supreme Court legalized abortion, giving women a decisive voice in a choice the court now deemed legitimate. I resumed my study, focusing on the decision of whether to continue or abort a pregnancy. I was totally blind to gender at the time, but what started as a study involving men became a study with women. And in that historical moment, following the Supreme Court ruling in Roe v. Wade, selflessness, long seen as the epitome of feminine goodness, suddenly appeared morally problematic. It signified an abdication of voice and an evasion of responsibility and relationship.

Listening to women, I was struck over and over again by the power of the opposition between selfishness and selflessness to shape women's moral judgments and guide the choices they made. I would hear women call whatever they wanted to do (whether to have the baby or have an abortion) "selfish," while describing doing what others wanted them to do as good. I remember Nina telling me that she was planning to have an abortion because her boyfriend wanted to finish law school and counted on her support. When I asked what she wanted to do, she said: "What's wrong with doing something for someone you love?" Nothing, I said, and repeated my question. After several iterations of this conversation, with the word "selfish" ringing in my ears, I began asking women: If it's good to be empathic

21

with people and responsive to their needs, why is it
selfish to respond to yourself? And in that historical
moment, woman after woman said: "Good question."

Listening to women thus led me to make a distinction I have come to see as pivotal to understanding
care ethics. Within a *patriarchal* framework, care is a
feminine ethic. Within a *democratic* framework, care
is a human ethic. A feminist ethic of care is a different
voice within a patriarchal culture because it joins reason
with emotion, mind with body, self with relationships,
men with women, resisting the divisions that maintain
a patriarchal order. To borrow the anthropologist
Clifford Geertz's distinction between thin and thick
interpretations of cultures—or rather the psychologist
Niobe Way's use of these terms to contrast cultural
stereotypes or clichés with an analysis of the culture
itself—a feminist ethic of care rests on a thick rather
than thin understanding of democracy. A thin interpretation of democracy homogenizes differences in the
name of equality, whereas thick democracy rests on the
premise that different voices are integral to the vitality
of a democratic society.

To answer, then, the first question raised above: a
feminist ethic of care is embattled because feminism is
embattled. The culture wars in the U.S. have brought to
the surface longstanding tensions in American society
between the commitment to democratic institutions and
values and the continuation of patriarchal privilege and
power. The gains made in the 1960s and '70s toward
realizing the promise of a truly democratic society
included direct challenges to patriarchal constructions

of masculinity and femininity on the part of the anti-war movement, the women's movement, and the gay liberation movement. To be a man did not necessarily mean becoming a soldier or preparing oneself for war; to be a woman did not necessitate becoming a mother or preparing oneself to bear and raise children. Both sexualities and families could take many forms. Yet abortion and gay marriage along with war remain to this day lightning-rod issues in American politics.

This brings me back to a major point: care and caring are not women's issues, they are human concerns. Until we make explicit the gendered nature of the justice vs. care debate, we will continue to be mystified by its seeming intransigence. And we will not move forward in dealing with the real questions of how concerns about fairness and rights intersect with concerns about care and responsibility. The moral injunction—do not oppress, do not exercise power unfairly or take advantage of others—lives side by side with the moral injunction to not abandon, to not act carelessly or neglect people who need help, meaning everyone including oneself. But they draw on different aspects of ourselves. Fairness and rights are matters of rules and principles. The logic is clear. If women are persons and persons have rights, then women have rights. Caring requires paying attention, seeing, listening, responding with respect. Its logic is contextual, psychological. Care is a relational ethic, grounded in a premise of interdependence. But it is not selfless.

To see the justice vs. care debate for what it is, look through a gender lens: justice is aligned with reason, mind, and self—the attributes of "rational

man"—and caring with emotion, body, and relationships—"feminine" concerns that like women in
patriarchy are at once idealized and devalued. Care then
becomes a subsidiary of justice, a matter of "special
obligations" or interpersonal relationships. Although
the patriarchal frame is not acknowledged, the gender
binaries and hierarchies catch the listening ear. With
this gendering of morality, manhood can readily become
a license for carelessness (defended in the name of rights
or freedom) and womanhood can imply a willingness to
forgo rights for the sake of preserving relationships and
keeping the peace. But it is absurd to say that men don't
care or that women are not invested in justice.

The different voice, then, is identified not by gender
but by theme. Its difference arises from joining reason
with emotion, self with relationships. Undoing patriarchal splits and hierarchies, it articulates democratic
norms and values: the importance of everyone having
a voice, being listened to carefully, and heard with
respect. The association of a care voice with women
was an empirical observation, admitting exceptions and
by no means limited to women, but for reasons I will
go into, women are more apt to resist separating themselves from relationships. To give just one illustration, a
medical student, when asked "How would you describe
yourself to yourself?" says,

> This sounds sort of strange, but I think maternal, with
> all its connotations. I see myself in a nurturing role,
> maybe not right now, but whenever that might be, as a
> physician, as a mother . . . It's hard to think of myself
> without thinking about other people . . .

She does not lack a sense of self, but she hears it as "strange" to describe herself as connecting with others rather than standing apart from them. In this way, she alerts us to a culture in which the self is presumed to be separate and to the difference between her response and a voice that says, "I would describe myself as an enthusiastic, passionate person who is slightly arrogant. Concerned, committed, very tired right now because I didn't get much sleep last night." Different voices. One mentions relationships in describing the self, one does not.

When the relational woman is judged to be good and the autonomous man is perceived as a principled moral agent, morality becomes aligned with and enforces the gender codes of a patriarchal order. In the culture of patriarchy (whether overt or hidden), the different voice with its ethic of care sounds feminine. Heard in its own right and on its own terms, it is a human voice. Listening to children, we hear the moral conviction in their cries "It's not fair" and "You don't care." Given that children are less powerful than adults and rely on the latter's care for their survival, concerns about justice and care are built into the human life cycle. The potential for oppression (using power unfairly) and for abandonment (acting carelessly) inheres in relationships, and an ethic of care speaks to these concerns.

When children are initiated into cultures that divide reason from emotion, mind from body, self from relationships, when these splits become tied to gender identity and the roles they are expected to play, they will feel pressed to reject or dissociate themselves from aspects of themselves that would lead them to appear

25

unmanly or not what a woman should be. At seventeen, Gail reflects, "I have a tendency to keep things to myself, things that bother me, and anything that interrupted my sense of what I should be, I would kind of soak up into myself, as though I was a big sponge." A high school senior, Fernando, one of the boys in Niobe Way's studies of boys' friendships and described in her book *Deep Secrets*, speaks about becoming a man. Asked what he sees as an ideal friendship, he says,

> You gotta be funny, truthful, I just got to have fun with you, you know. I just don't want to get tired of you right away. 'Cause if I get tired of you, you are not really my friend. Um, you gotta, I guess just be there for me? I guess, I don't wanna sound too sissy-like . . . I think I've matured in certain ways . . . I know how to be more of a man. (p. 242)

Gail has learned to soak up anger (her own and that of others) in order to be "what I should be," and Fernando, in learning how to be a man, has learned to regard wanting others to be there for him as "sissy-like."

The initiation into patriarchy is driven by gender and enforced by shaming and exclusion. Its telltale signs are a loss of voice and memory, an inability to tell one's story accurately. Thus the initiation of children into a patriarchal order leaves a legacy of loss and some of the scars we have come to associate with trauma. Twelve-year-old Becka, one of the girls described in *Meeting at the Crossroads* (Lyn Mikel Brown and my book on girls' development), speaks of losing her sense of herself:

> I wasn't being happy, and I wasn't sure of myself . . .
> I wasn't being . . . with myself and I wasn't thinking

about myself. I just wanted to have this group of friends
. . . I was losing confidence in myself, I was losing track
of myself really, and losing the kind of person I was.
(p. 167)

As a high school junior, Nick, another of the boys in
Way's studies, speaks of losing his friends:

Friendships were actually more important when I was
a kid because I—always needed friends . . . Um, I feel
like, sort of sad that they are gone. But the friends that
I have now, you know, we try to make the best of it.
You know, like I said, friends do come and go but the
friends that you have now, you try to make the best of
it. (p. 155)

It is not surprising then that at times in development
when children are initiated into the codes and scripts of
patriarchal manhood and womanhood—times when it
becomes essential for boys to act like "real boys" and
for girls to become "good girls," when those who do
not are shamed, beaten, excluded, mocked, shunned
and condemned—it is not surprising that these times
in development are marked by signs of psychological distress. Among boys between the ages of five and
seven, the age when boys who cross gender boundaries
are called girls or gay or sissies or mama's boys, there
is a high incidence of learning and speech disorders,
attention problems, and out of touch and out of control behavior. Boys show more signs of depression
than girls until adolescence, the time when the division
between good and bad girls sets in, enforced by often
vicious practices of inclusion and exclusion. At adolescence, there is a heightened risk to girls' resilience,

reflected in a suddenly increased incidence among girls of depression, eating disorders, cutting and other forms of destructive behavior. In the late years of high school, around sixteen or seventeen—the time when Nick says, "I'm not close to anybody now"—the suicide rate rises sharply among boys, as does the rate of homicide.

Looking at such experiences, it becomes easier to understand the tenacity of patriarchy, even in societies committed to democratic institutions and values. The structures of domination become invisible because they have been internalized. Incorporated into the psyche, they appear not as manifestations of culture but as part of nature—part of us.

In the theories of Freud, Erikson, Piaget, Kohlberg, and their contemporary offshoots in psychoanalysis and cognitive psychology, the separation of the self from relationships and the elevation of mind over body, reason over emotion, appear as milestones along a developmental path, markers of progress toward maturity. The splits themselves have become naturalized and mistaken for development, or seen as a requisite of civilization. The loss of relationship suffered along the way is deemed necessary, part of the price we pay for growing up. The hand of patriarchy remains hidden in these accounts of development until suddenly it appears unmistakably: morality and development itself are premised on the internalization of the voice or law of the father.

In the first meeting Judy Chu and I have with the fathers of the four- and five-year-old boys we are observing, Alex takes the lead, the winter sky dark outside the windows of the school library. He speaks about Nick, his five-year-old son, being "out there"—emotionally open, vulnerable, exposed. The room becomes quiet as he continues:

> He's out there, he needs to really be out there, and I always feel, it's always tricky how much you want to clamp down on him. And clamp down in the sense that he was getting into all sorts of trouble at school ... I always think about it, there's spunk there ... he's very spunky, and I hate for that to be squeezed out of him. As I believe it was squeezed out of me, you know, I was exactly like that.

"And you remember your spunk?" I ask him, wondering about the word, its sexual overtones, its evocation of life and joy. "Yeah," he says. "How did you lose it?" I wonder. Alex hesitates. "I think I just got into trouble so much in school ... I remember, I think it took me until about tenth grade to figure that out." It is as if he is fighting with memory as he speaks of having been good enough in school, getting good grades, "but every now and then I would remember, you know"—he breaks the sentence, then picks it up—"There'd be a parent–teacher conference where, you know, 'This kid is out of control, there's too much energy here,' or something like that." He recalls the words of his parents and teachers, but for himself, this otherwise very articulate man seems to be at a loss for words or to have no words for what he remembers—a sensation perhaps, a spirit rising, a liveliness that became linked with being "out of control" or having "too much energy." "I just became good," Alex says, "and decided, you know, to study hard and blend into the crowd, and go to track practice, that was it."

Tom, another father, interjects, "That sucked up the energy." But Alex continues on his train of thought: "And it was, it's sad." Speaking of his five-year-old son, he says, "I really don't want that to happen to him." "So what's the negative?" asks Michael, another father; "What did you lose?" Illustrating his point with his manner, Alex says matter-of-factly, "I think I lost my spunk."

Alex is a professor, tenured at an early age at a prestigious university. He has separated from his wife; he is trying to become more connected with his children. He is a man struggling with issues that many men struggle with—how to be a good man, a father, how not to repeat his father's patterns, how to live with himself and with women, how to raise a son and a daughter. And doing this from a position of advantage: he is high up on the patriarchal ladder, and he wants the best for his children. Which is where the quandary enters: Alex fears that Nick will walk the same path he has, and also that Nick will fall off that path. What Michael cherishes in his son Gabe, the qualities he sees that lead him to say "I hope he never loses that," are "his sensitivity," his "real joy" and the "delight he has in his friends." The sadness that blanches Michael's face suggests that joy and close friendships are things he now longs for.

In *Essays on the History of Ethics*, Michael Slote, a moral philosopher, highlights the advantages of integrating a philosophical with a psychological understanding of morality. In place of the usual distinctions philosophers make between Kantian (golden rule), utilitarian (greatest good), and Aristotelian or virtue ethics, he posits a psychological spectrum for moral theory, a continuum leading from separateness to connectedness. He finds this ordering at once more comprehensive and more explanatory of the differences in moral theories. Although he does not state it in these terms, he is advocating a paradigm shift, a reframing of moral theory in the light of care ethics.

Along the same lines, when Barack Obama grounded his campaign for the presidency in a call for "change we can believe in," he was calling for a different voice. The response galvanized by this call captured the yearning for a new conversation to replace ones that were going nowhere. The hope aroused was audacious. Exhilaration filled the streets of New York on the night of his election, suggesting the release of energy that accompanies the move out of dissociation. Obama had encouraged us to know what we knew about the war in Iraq, about social justice, about the state of the economy, the country, our lives. On the night he received his party's nomination he promised he would tell us the truth and listen to those who disagreed with him. The shift from the patriarchal manhood of George W. Bush ("the decider") to the more democratic manhood of Barack Obama was palpable. And some of the disillusionment that has followed may reflect the disappointment in finding ourselves still mired in old battles, with less transparency than we had expected and less change than we had anticipated. Although dissections of Obama's presidency have not zeroed in on issues of gender, his manhood has been questioned across the political spectrum, with Dick Cheney calling him "dithering" and "weak" and critics on the left faulting him for not standing up to the military and Wall Street. As a political scientist friend observed, health care, gendered feminine, is considered too expensive and not the government's responsibility, while the military budget and Wall Street, gendered masculine, have gotten a relatively free pass. Perhaps we had believed that democracy would trump patriarchy at last.

The paradigm shift in the human sciences casts new light on these matters of gender. We were accustomed to seeing ourselves (or at least the men among us) as aggressive and competitive by nature, engaged whether rationally or irrationally in the pursuit of self-interest. The emerging consensus, reflected by the number of books now appearing with the word "empathy" or "cooperation" in their titles (*The Age of Empathy*, *The Empathic Civilization*, *Why We Cooperate*, etc.), portrays us as inherently empathic and cooperative beings, harboring within ourselves the capacity to love and to live democratically with others. Titling his book *Together*, the sociologist Richard Sennett underscores the difficulty of cooperation in a competitive world. The psychologist's question—my question—is what happens then to our capacity for empathy and cooperation, how do we lose our humanity? Or do we?

I come then to my final question: Why women? Are women's voices still key in freeing democracy from the vestiges of patriarchy? I will argue that the issue is not one of essentialism or socialization, but one of development and initiation. It is not that women are essentially different from men or are all the same, or that men and women are socialized to play different roles, which is often the case. Instead, like a healthy body, a healthy psyche resists disease. There is an inherent tension between our human nature and the structures of patriarchy, leading the healthy psyche to resist an initiation that mandates a loss of voice and a sacrifice of relationship. It fights for freedom from dissociation, from the splits in consciousness that would keep parts of ourselves and our experience outside our awareness. How else would women have found the will to secure agency, property ownership, the vote, fair pay, and freedom, including freeing themselves from what Lyn Mikel Brown and I called "the tyranny of nice and kind?" How would any people free themselves from psychological as well as political colonization?

The neurobiologist Antonio Damasio tells us that we register our experience from moment to moment. In our bodies and our emotions, we pick up the music or "the feeling of what happens." When we fail to record these signals in our minds and thoughts, our thoughts become divorced from our experience and we can readily fall under the sway of false authority. The grounds for love and for democracy slip away from under our feet.

In the early 1980s, following the completion of *In a Different Voice*, I began a study of girls' development to fill in what was at the time a missing stretch of psychological history. Joseph Adelson, editor of the 1980 *Handbook of Adolescent Psychology*, had observed that girls had "simply not been much studied," and that the psychology of adolescence contained a "subtle but unmistakable masculine bias," leading to an over-emphasis on achievement, independence, and separation and a corresponding neglect of nurturance, intimacy, and relationships. Girls' experiences in coming of age, a subject for playwrights and novelists, had remained for the most part unexplored by psychologists, and a masculine bias had led them to overlook the more "feminine" aspects of boys' lives.

Knowing this, it becomes more apparent why eleven-year-old Amy's voice was unsettling to many readers of *In a Different Voice.* It was a voice they had learned to silence or disparage, preferring the clarity of eleven-year-old Jake to what they heard as Amy's equivocation. Responding to the question of whether a man named Heinz whose wife was dying of cancer should steal an overpriced drug to save her life, Jake says that he should because property is replaceable but life is not ("You couldn't get Heinz's wife again."). In contrast, Amy says,

> Well, I don't think so. I think there might be other ways beside stealing it, like if he could borrow the money or make a loan or something, but he really shouldn't steal the drug—but his wife shouldn't die either.

Asked why he shouldn't steal the drug, she says,

> If he stole the drug, he might save her life then, but if he did, he might have to go to jail, and then his wife might get sicker again, and he couldn't get more of the drug, and it might not be good. So, they should really just talk it out and find some other way to make the money.

There are many things one can notice in her response having to do with social class, the justice system, the active role she accords the unnamed wife in the decision making, and the narrative form her reasoning takes. But most striking perhaps is the recognition that Amy was not answering the interviewer's question. The woman interviewing her had asked: "*Should* Heinz steal the drug?" (Would stealing be right or wrong?) whereas to Amy the question was: "Should Heinz *steal* the drug?" (Is stealing the best thing to do?). Suddenly her answer makes sense. There might, as she says, be better ways to solve this problem. Amy's voice is unsettling because she gives voice to something that rings true to experience but is at odds with what has been socially constructed as reality or morality. The research on girls' development exposed this gap between experience and a socially constructed reality.

A cardinal finding lay in the observation that, at the brink of adolescence, girls speak of feeling pressed to choose between having a voice and having relationships, a choice that psychologically makes no sense. To silence oneself and not say what one is thinking and feeling is to forgo relationship—to give up on the possibility of living in connection with others. Conversely, in the absence of resonance, voice recedes into silence. Over and over again, my colleagues and I heard girls describe a crisis of relationship. Experiences of connectedness which up to that time had seemed ordinary and which they had taken for granted suddenly were called into question. Entering secondary education and becoming young women, they were encouraged to separate their minds from their bodies, their thoughts from their emotions, their honest voices from their relationships. In a variety of subtle and not so subtle ways, they were discouraged from saying what they saw or listening to what they heard. In coming of age, girls had to fend off pressures to silence themselves, paradoxically for the sake of having relationships.

My colleagues and I listened as girls named the various inducements held out and the rewards to be gained by keeping their thoughts and feelings to themselves. They were reading the culture in which they were coming of age, a culture uneasy about adolescent girls connecting with their bodies, where women's desires and emotions are often suspect. We saw girls align themselves with the more highly valued masculine traits and denigrate other girls and women. Yet what struck me most in the course of this research were the clarity of girls' honest voices and the tenacity of their resistance to silencing themselves for the sake of what they recognized to be a chimera of relationship. Even when succumbing to the pressures of initiation, articulate girls would narrate their experience and reflect on what was happening to them. The move into womanhood threatened to confuse their sense of what is true or real. In a conversation about whether it is ever good to tell a lie, eleven-year-old Elise, a fifth-grader in an urban public school, observes: "My house is wallpapered with lies."

The following incident sums up the key developmental finding of the research. At the end of a five-year longitudinal, cross-sectional study involving nearly a hundred girls between the ages of seven and eighteen, diverse in ethnicity and social class background but having in common educational advantage, I go to speak with the girls to tell them how their voices are affecting women and men and to ask how they want to be involved now that my colleagues and I are presenting our findings and preparing to publish them in a book

(*Meeting at the Crossroads*). The thirteen-year-olds respond without hesitation: "We want you to tell them everything we said, and we want our names in the book!" When I ask if they want their names next to excerpts from their interviews or at the front of the book, Tracy, perhaps anticipating how her nine-year-old self might be heard, says, "When we were nine, we were stupid." I say it would never have occurred to me to use the word "stupid" because what struck me most about them when they were nine was how much they knew. At which point Tracy says, "I mean, when we were nine, we were honest." Between nine and thirteen, an honest voice had come to seem or to sound stupid.

And yet it is a voice girls resist losing.

Beginning in the mid-nineteenth century and continuing into the present, psychiatrists and psychologists have noted that girls' resilience is at heightened risk during adolescence, a risk commonly attributed to the effects of hormones or socialization. Listening to girls, my colleagues and I came instead to see their resilience as compromised when they find they must silence their honest voices in order to be accepted and loved. What is socially adaptive is psychologically costly and ultimately politically costly as well. The sacrifice of voice and relationships compromises psychological health and also the viability of a democratic society.

The ability of girls to articulate their initiation into the gendered splits and hierarchies that constitute and maintain a patriarchal order gives voice to a problem that is not simply a problem for girls. Taking in how astutely girls can read the human world around them, I found myself—the mother of boys—thinking: boys do this too. Yet the initiation of boys into a masculinity where being a boy means not being like a girl and also being dominant, typically occurs earlier in development, when they don't yet have the range of experience and the cognitive capacities they will gain at adolescence. Little boys are equally astute in reading the human emotional world, including emotions that are being withheld: "Mama, why do you smile when you are sad?" five-year-old Tony asks. And when Alex, Nick's father, expresses his remorse for having "lost it" and hit Nick the previous day, Nick says to his father, "You are afraid that if you hit me, when I grow up I'll hit my children." Alex had been hit by his father and had vowed to break the cycle. Five-year-old Nick picks up his fear that the cycle will now continue into the next generation.

At four and five, children are learning how things are. At adolescence, with secondary education and higher order thinking (the ability to think about thinking), they learn how things are said to be: how we talk about things, what is the right way to speak and to be. When it comes to issues of gender, girls tend to be given more leeway than boys up until adolescence, when they reach reproductive maturity. Just think of a boy coming to school in a dress. At adolescence, boys become more reflective, but when the shock of initiation hits girls at adolescence, they can more readily say what boys cannot openly express without casting doubts on their manhood.

We begin to understand why girls and women are key in exposing patriarchal structures, why they can play a leading role in transforming patriarchal into democratic practices. For reasons having to do with the later timing of their initiation, they can more readily give voice to aspects of human experience that otherwise tend to remain unspoken or unseen. But we can also understand the pressures on girls when they reach adolescence not to say what they are seeing or know what they know and to cede an honest voice in the interest of having relationships and getting ahead in the world.

Our studies of girls' development extended for over ten years in a range of school and after-school settings and illuminated a trajectory of resistance. A healthy resistance to losses that are psychologically costly takes on the characteristics of a political resistance when girls speak truth to power. At fifteen, Amy responds to the Heinz dilemma by telling her interviewer "the situation is unreal." Where would the cancer drug be, she asks, on a shelf in a drugstore? "I have a lot of trouble buying that story," she says. When told by the camp director that her homesick cousin cannot call his parents because it is against the rules, Shaunya tells him, "Sorry, but he's only seven. People are more important than rules." When this open resistance can find no effective channel for expression, it may go underground and be held in silence, or it may become dissociated and held out of awareness, turning into a psychological resistance, a reluctance to know what one knows.

The later timing of girls' encounter with the systemic enforcement of patriarchal gender codes and mores also means that girls' resistance tends to be closer to consciousness and more accessible to recovery, whether through the associative patterns of memory and artistic endeavors or through shifts in societal and cultural resonances. To say that violence occurs when women's voices are silent or silenced does not mean that women are not or cannot be violent. As a generalization, it is true that girls are more schooled in relationships, more adept in the processes of rupture and repair, and that violence itself is gendered masculine, associated with militarism and with honor. But the critical importance of women's voices lies in the recognition that for a variety of reasons, women are more likely to recognize and name the patriarchal story as a false story. It is a story so patently false in its representation of women and men (it's nonsense to say that women don't think or men don't feel, or that women have relationships and men have selves) that the question becomes: why are these gender stereotypes so persistent and why do we repeat them?

To return then to where I began, what stands in the way of listening to women? What keeps a woman from saying what she really feels and thinks? When I was interviewing pregnant women about abortion decisions, Larry Kohlberg, at that point my colleague on the faculty, had his Harvard class vote on whether abortion is a moral dilemma. He reported that they voted it was not because the fetus doesn't have rights. I remember thinking: so, women were talking about nothing? There was no moral issue? What struck me at the time and still does today is the dissonance between the ways I heard and continue to hear women wrestle with the ethical issues involved in choosing whether to continue or abort a pregnancy and the terms of the public abortion debate. For many women, the overriding ethical questions have less to do with whether or not the fetus has rights in some abstract moral universe and more to do with how to resolve conflicts of responsibility and care. Yet it remains difficult for a woman to raise these concerns within the framework of the rights debate without being misheard or misunderstood, at worst called a murderer, or else told she is making a fuss over nothing.

In writing *In a Different Voice*, I became starkly aware that if I listened to the voices of women I would be challenging the voices of authority. I framed the argument of my book as a syllogism: if women's voices differ from the voice of psychological and moral theory, is the problem in women or in the theory? My answer was both: there was a problem in theory—a need for a different voice—and this in turn created a problem for women and men living in a world where the reigning constructions of reality and morality did not jibe with their experience—a world where it was necessary for a woman to learn to think in a way that differed from the way she really thought if she wanted to be heard and understood. Bringing women's voices into what was then called the human conversation changed the voice of that conversation by shifting the paradigm, changing the frame. Like a sound piercing a silence, women's voices broke through a collective not knowing or dissociation. Once women were speaking more openly about their experiences, including their experiences of incest and other forms of abuse, it became easier for men to speak about their experiences of violation, leading to the exposure of the widespread priest sexual abuse scandal.

In *The Birth of Pleasure*, I raise the question: why are we so drawn to tragic love stories? and suggest it is because they tell a story we know and have to understand, a trauma story we otherwise tend to repeat. The tragic love story is the quintessential story of patriarchy—the story of Abraham and Isaac, Jepthe and his daughter, Agamemnon and Iphigenia. It conveys a willingness on the part of fathers to sacrifice love for the sake of hierarchy and honor, but also, more subtly, the recognition that love is the enemy of patriarchy, crossing its boundaries, dissolving its hierarchies, and thus challenging its most fundamental assumptions about how things are and how things have to be. Think of *West Side Story* or *Romeo and Juliet*. We know now that the failure to care leads to an inability to care and that the antithesis of voice is violence.

In the years since I wrote *In a Different Voice*, research in the human sciences has changed our understanding of the human condition. In *The Age of Empathy* (2010), the primatologist Frans de Waal calls for "a complete overhaul of assumptions about human nature" (p. 7), noting that these assumptions have been skewed by the emphasis on competition and aggression. His research provides extensive evidence of the empathic nature of primates including humans, and scientists more generally now speak of "emotional intelligence," the "relational self," and the "feeling brain." The old gender binaries are coming undone. But in this changing conversation, a history tends to be lost or rewritten: these insights came initially from listening to women who joined reason with emotion, self with relationship, mind with body. In an age of climate change, pandemics, and nuclear weapons, interdependence has become self-evident. And with this recognition, it becomes obvious, as Patricia Papperman writes, that "There is nothing exceptional about vulnerable people." Vulnerability, once associated with women, is a characteristic of humans.

Looking forward then, we can expect a struggle. As long as the different voice sounds different, the tensions between democracy and patriarchy continue. Once the ethic of care is released from its subsidiary position within a justice framework, it can guide us by framing the struggle in a way that clarifies what is at stake and by illuminating a path of resistance grounded not in ideology but in our humanity. If along the path we lose our way, we can remind ourselves to listen for voice, to pay attention to how things are gendered, and to remember that within ourselves we have the ability to spot a false story.

2 Where Have We Come From and Where Are We Going?

A Fable

In a certain university, in a certain department—but as Gogol writes, "I had better not mention which department. There is nothing more touchy than a department"—in a certain year (let's say mid-way through the 1990s), the following events took place. It was the fall, and early in the term, a Student came to her adviser, the Professor. The Student had been in the masters program the previous year, and the Professor knew her as a high-spirited young woman: passionate, intelligent, radiant. Yet the woman who entered her office that day was pale and subdued. "What happened?" the Professor asked. "Haven't you heard?" the Student replied. The Professor had not.

The Student proceeded to tell the Professor what was going on in the pro-seminar, the overview course mandatory for first-year doctoral students and taught by the department Chair. Another student in the class had objected to the absence of readings on women's

44

psychology. Contention broke out over whether or not this was a problem. Apparently, the Chair advised the objector (a woman who then became known as "the Feminist") that if she wanted to be a psychologist, she must choose an area of study central to the field. The Chair was not alone in her opinion. A colleague had advised a student (who was studying the epidemic of cutting among adolescent girls) not to use gender as a category of analysis if she did not want her research to be marginalized.

In any event, the issue was dropped in the pro-seminar, though not without repercussions. The Feminist, who had specified her intention to study women's psychology on her application, went to the Dean and asked for her money back. Others in the class who had looked on in silence registered their distress in their bodies. A Native American lesbian (called by the Cree "two-spirited") went home and threw up.

As the Student told the Professor this story, the Professor scanned the face of her student. It was listless, and her voice was full of resignation. The Professor thought about her own position within the department—whether or not to take the matter personally. She herself was somewhat marginalized in the department, but it had given her a kind of freedom, and as her Dean observed, she was running "a school within a school." In that spirit, she offered to meet with the disaffected students to read and discuss the books they wanted to study. And so, what came to be called the "underground pro-seminar" began, a series of weekly meetings held in the Professor's office, attended by five first-year doctoral students including the Feminist and the Native

American, and augmented by an effort at consciousness raising that took the form of a kind of street theater. Each week a "quotation of the week" appeared in the department elevator, with selections ranging from Audrey Lorde's "the master's tools will never dismantle the master's house" to the line from the end of *King Lear*: "Speak what you feel, not what you ought to say."

The semester progressed and, mid-way through the term, the Professor received a call from the Dean's office. The Visiting Committee had arrived, and two of its members had expressed a wish to sit in on her lecture class. She said they would be welcome and they came, sitting in the front row off to her left and staying awake for the entire two hours. Afterward, they rushed up to thank her, and when they spoke of their wish to learn more about the doctoral program, she asked if they would like to meet some students.

And so, on a rainy November morning, a woman from the Visiting Committee appeared in the underground pro-seminar (her friend who felt under the weather had stayed behind in the hotel). The Professor told the students that their Visitor wanted to hear about their experiences in the doctoral program, and a look of utter astonishment came over her face as they told her what had happened in the department pro-seminar. This was something the Visitor would never have imagined. Being the mother of an adolescent daughter, she had found the research on women and girls particularly informative.

Within a month, the Visitor had enlisted her friend and two other women, and the four of them pooled their resources to endow a chair in gender studies, the first such professorship in the university. The endowed chair would be located in the department and named, very appropriately, for a former Dean, the first woman ever to become a Dean at the university.

Twelve years passed. The listless Student, radiant again, graduated and eventually became tenured at an Ivy League university and the mother of two children. The Professor moved on to another university.

Then one day, in the spring of 2009, the Professor received an email from the Dean, the woman for whom the gender chair was named. The Professor had sent the Dean her new book, thinking its integration of psychology and history would interest her since history was the Dean's field. The Dean was writing to thank the Professor. The Dean recalled, as had the Professor, their many conversations about psychology and history and said she looked forward to reading the book.

The Dean added that the Professor would be interested to know that her former department Chair (the woman who had taught the pro-seminar) was about to become the new occupant of the chair named in the Dean's honor. She went on explain that the three donors who were still living had been consulted and they had agreed that the chair no longer needed to focus on gender.

The Professor was not surprised by the news that her former colleague had been awarded an endowed chair, although the irony of the appointment did not escape her. What surprised her was the willingness of the donors to remove the word "gender" from the name of the chair they had formerly endowed in order to legitimize gender as a field of study.

As you may have guessed, I was the Professor in this story, and what makes it a fable is that rather than the gender chair becoming part of the historical record, these events have been washed over, are no longer engraved, and now exist only as myth or legend. At the beginning of *Haroun and the Sea of Stories*, Salman Rushdie writes: "There was once . . . a city so ruinously sad that it had forgotten its name." At the end of the fable of the Feminist in the pro-seminar, the reason for the chair had similarly been forgotten.

Where have we come from and where are we going? I was reflecting on the lives of women, asking myself, Where are we now? when I heard the ambiguity in the pronoun "we." Like a tap from the unconscious, it cued what I wanted to say: namely, that women's lives are a beacon—or as Virginia Woolf might have it, a lighthouse—showing a path that we as humans have traveled and also a way leading forward. Women's voices can provide a resonance that may keep us from getting lost.

The changes in many women's lives over the past half-century followed from the recognition that women's rights are human rights, or, to put it more bluntly, from the discovery that women are in fact human. Still, you can't write a book called *In a Different Voice* without finding yourself in the midst of the argument over whether women are the same as men or different from them, and, if different, who is better (although these were not my questions in that book). I had heard a dissonance between women's voices and the voices that shaped psychological theory and public debate.

More personally, in listening to other women, I found a resonance for a voice I myself was holding in silence.

"Why is feminism still so divisive?" a 2009 cover headline in *The New Yorker* inquires. Reviewing two books on modern feminism, Ariel Levy begins by noting the distortions in the historical record: "it's as if feminism were plagued by a kind of false-memory syndrome." This "cultural memory disorder," she observes, has kept us from remembering the radical insight that the politics of equality are incompatible with the structure of the traditional family. The goal of full citizenship for women implied a societal transformation that would have "changed this country on a cellular level." Child care was the bone of contention:

> If the father works and the mother works, nobody is left to watch the kids. Either government acknowledges the situation and helps provide child care (as many European countries do), or child care becomes a luxury affordable by the affluent, and a major problem for everyone else.

The lines of division were predictable: feminism became identified with the interests of privileged, mostly white women, who then divided among themselves over whether it is possible to defend traditional structures and still call oneself a feminist—as Sarah Palin does—or whether feminism implies a transformation on a societal level.

To illustrate the depths of our collective false memory, Levy summons a startling fact:

> In 1971, a bipartisan group of senators, led by Walter Mondale, came up with legislation that would have

established both early-education programs and after-school care across the country. Tuition would be on a sliding scale based on a family's income bracket, and the program would be available to everyone but participation was required of no one. Both houses of Congress passed the bill.

Nobody remembers this because, later that year,

President Nixon vetoed the Comprehensive Child Development Act, declaring that it "would commit the vast moral authority of the National Government on the side of communal approaches to child-rearing" and undermine the "family-centered approach." He meant "the traditional family-centered approach," which requires women to forsake every ambition apart from motherhood.

By focusing on representation with one woman as good as another—Sarah Palin or Hillary Clinton—feminism "lost its larger ambitions." The conservatives co-opted its radical agenda by focusing on the family. A federal program ensuring that women with school-age children would have affordable child care thus became a dream (or a nightmare, as Nixon thought) rather than an accomplishment.

Yet while the culture wars were raging, the paradigm in the human sciences was changing. Holding up the icon of the traditional family—the nuclear family, the Oedipal family—psychology along with biology and anthropology had been implicated in the road not taken. They had bestowed scientific sanction on the trinity of the father, the mother, and the child. In the 1970s, a new breed of researchers that included more women began asking new questions and gathering new evidence that dislodged many seemingly rock-solid assumptions about human nature and human development. Quietly or not so quietly, books appeared with titles announcing a change in the framework: *Toward a New Psychology of Women* (1976), *In a Different Voice* (1982), *The Mismeasure of Man* (1982), *The Interpersonal World of the Infant* (1986), *Descartes' Error* (1994), *The Birth of Pleasure* (2002), and in 2010, *Mothers and Others: The Evolutionary Origins of Mutual Understanding*. A growing body of evidence from a variety of disciplines could not be accommodated by the old frameworks.

I. Where have we come from?

According to Sarah Blaffer Hrdy, an evolutionary anthropologist, what distinguishes us from our Great Ape ancestors is our capacity for mutual understanding. At a very early point in development, practically from birth, human babies scan faces, make eye-contact, and engage the attention of others. An NYU colleague noted that he could see this most days on the subway. Babies display the rudiments of a finely tuned empathy, an ability to read others' intentions, a desire for connection with others, attentiveness to their responses, and curiosity about their emotions. Given her evolutionary standpoint, Hrdy's question is: Where does this come from?

The answer, she finds, lies in alloparenting, meaning simply the engagement of others who are not the biological parents in the raising of a child. The conditions of early hominid existence made it essential for someone in addition to the mother to invest in the child's survival. Since mutual understanding facilitates alloparenting, "babies who were better at gauging the intentions of others and engaging with them were also better at eliciting care and hence more likely to survive into adulthood and reproduce" (*Mothers and Others*, p. 117). Evolution selected for those qualities that facilitate mutual understanding: empathy, mind-reading, and cooperation. The absence in children of these central and almost defining human qualities can be seen in the devastating developmental deficiency called autism.

Hrdy conceived her book *Mothers and Others* as "one long argument" against those who subscribe to the "man as hunter" hypothesis, which had assumed pride of place as an explanation of "the prodigious adaptation central to the success of early hominids" (p. 147). At the heart of this model is a "sex contract": a "pact between a hunter who provided for his mate and a mate who repaid him with sexual fidelity so the provider could be certain that the children he invested in carried at least half of his genes" (p. 147). A series of discoveries coming from studies of primates and observations of people who actually live by hunting and gathering led researchers to conclude that although the hunting hypothesis describes family life among our Great Ape ancestors, it does not apply to our hominid forebears. "The continuous contact between mother and infant that seemed so self-evident and so natural to [John] Bowlby, as well as to Darwin," turns out to be a projection, perhaps unconscious, of "pre-conceived Western ideals of how a mother *should* care for her infant"

(p. 84). In reality, the evidence suggests that without alloparenting or communal child-rearing, "there never would have been a human species" (p. 109). It is not the nuclear family and exclusive maternal care but the capacity for mutual understanding and extended families that are coded into our genes.

Hrdy's discoveries remove a blinder that has kept us from seeing what is right before our eyes. I grew up with an alloparent, my father's father, who lived with us not in a hunter-gatherer society but in a New York apartment. As a mother, I relied on a network of others: my parents, neighbors and friends. A glance at the Obama White House reveals an alloparent (Michelle's mother) in residence, and Obama himself, raised by his mother and others (her mother and father), displays the capacity for mutual understanding along with ambition and leadership—qualities researchers now find to be associated with alloparenting. The ideal environment for raising children turns out to be not that of the nuclear family but one in which there are at least three secure relationships (gender nonspecific), meaning three relationships that convey the clear message: "You will be cared for no matter what."

In a law school seminar on resisting injustice, in the week we were reading Sarah Hrdy, a woman recalls the time when her nomadic nuclear family moved to Iowa where they knew no one. She remembers being terror-struck at the thought that should something happen to her parents and sister, no one would know where to send her. Her terror could only be assuaged by her mother knocking on the door of a neighbor, then a complete stranger, to ask if she would promise to send

53

Megan to her grandparents in Texas should something happen to the rest of them. But Megan was an exception; in this group of twenty-two law students, only three had grown up without alloparents.

To psychoanalysts, the function of the third in the Oedipal triangle is to break up the couple of mother and child. To Hrdy and like-minded socio-biologists, the third functions not to separate mother and child but to enhance the child's capacity for empathy and set up expectations about the social world that will facilitate subsequent relationships. It is a lesson learned by resilient children who, in the face of nuclear or other family dysfunction, seek out the person or persons in the environment (the grandparent, the upstairs neighbor, the aunt, the brother's girlfriend, the housekeeper) who is able to care for them.

The blinder was the traditional family, the holy family, photographs of baby chimps clinging to mothers who warn others away, the endless representations of doe-eyed Madonnas alone with their infants, the family of the hunting hypothesis, the family structured around a gender binary and hierarchy where being a father means not being a mother and also being the voice of authority. In reality, human mothers, in contrast to their chimp counterparts, turn their babies to face outward and under normal conditions hand them around for others to hold and engage with—something no chimp mother would dream of doing. In calling her book *Mothers and Others*, Hrdy signals what is at stake. The missing word, "fathers," conveys her intention of "ushering in a new way of thinking about family life among our ancestors" (p. 109). The alloparenting model displaces the patriarchal family by showing it to be neither traditional nor original in an evolutionary sense. As Hrdy says, "This is revolutionary stuff" (p. 7).

A different voice, a new way of thinking about self and morality, of imagining relationships, of thinking about family life. This is what is meant by a paradigm shift. Once the paradigm shifts, it becomes difficult to see or listen in the old way. It changes "what being human means" (p. 7).

Hrdy goes to some lengths to make clear she is not talking about "father absence," regarded as a blight on the nuclear family. Fathers are present in her model. The photographs in her book that stopped me show a father smiling with an infant asleep on his chest and a man sitting on the ground in a circle of children. They capture men's tenderness and quiet attentiveness. They moved me and also surprised me in the sense that although I know this to be true about men—knew it as a child with my father and grandfather, know it as a wife and a mother of sons—it is not how men appear in portraits of manhood. The photographs have a candid quality, as if catching men off guard.

In an article published in the journal *Neuron* ("A Neural Basis for Social Cooperation"), James Rilling and his colleagues report that our brains light up more brightly when we choose cooperative over competitive strategies—and in the same area of the brain lit up by chocolate. The research subjects were women, and the researchers wonder if they would find similar results among CEOs. As Hrdy points out, responsive fathers, "extra-fathers," nurturing uncles and other such men retain the human capacity for mutual understanding and enhance a child's development. Holding an infant or caring for young children affects men as well as women on a hormonal level, reducing testosterone and increasing the circulating levels of prolactin (a hormone shown to promote nurturing responses in mammals and other species). We know that humans can be selfish and cruel, competitive over resources and mates. The revolutionary insight is that by nature we are cooperative, relational beings, and our capacity for mutual understanding is linked to the survival of our species.

Reading Hrdy, I understood more clearly what had moved me most deeply in reading John Bowlby's book *Loss* and Robert Coles's *Children of Crisis*. It was the descriptions of grandmothers accompanying their grandchildren through the sorrows of loss and the integration of schools. The grandmothers were the alloparents, and Hrdy was right: they were responsible for the child's survival.

By the end of the twentieth century, the hunting hypothesis had "effectively collapsed" (p. 149). Yet it continues to be promulgated by researchers and politicians, and remains in leading universities "a centerpiece of the teaching curriculum." Hrdy cites a 2004 textbook, written by two Harvard professors, who "take for granted that 'monogamous pair-bonding and nuclear families were dominant throughout human history in hunter gatherer societies'" (p. 148). In 2003, the U.S. president, speaking the voice of the decider, declared: "studies have shown that the ideal is where a child is raised in a married family with a man and a woman." Hrdy's personal library is filled with books having titles like *Life Without Father: Compelling Evidence*

Where Have We Come From and Where Are We Going?

That Fatherhood and Marriage Are Indispensible for the Good of Children and for Society or *Fatherless in America: Confronting Our Most Urgent Social Problem*, books written by sociologists of the family who,

> without asking under what historical or economic or social conditions this will be so, take for granted that "children develop best when they are provided with the opportunity to have warm, intimate, continuous and enduring relationships with both their fathers and their mothers." (p. 145)

This could be written off as yet another academic skirmish except for its social policy implications, its impact on the lives of women, and the fact that from an evolutionary standpoint, as Hrdy notes, "patriarchal ideologies that focused on both the chastity of women and the perpetuation and augmentation of male lineages undercut the long-standing priority of putting children's well-being first" (p. 287). One has only to think of poor Oedipus—slated for extinction in order to preserve the life of his father and surviving only through the intervention of shepherds, the alloparents who rescue him and take him to Corinth—to see her point.

II. Where have we come to?

If the writings of *New York Times* op-ed columnists are an indication, two books published in 2009 place women at the forefront. In *When Everything Changed: The Amazing Journey of American Women from 1960 to the Present*, Gail Collins reports the "astonishing revolution" that led women from having to obtain their husbands' permission to apply for a credit card to running for president of the United States, not to mention running in marathons and becoming astronauts, construction workers, and university presidents. In *Half the Sky: Turning Oppression into Opportunity for Women Worldwide*, Nicholas Kristoff and Sheryl WuDunn sound "a passionate call to take up arms against the leading human rights violation of our era: the oppression of women and girls in the developing world." Taken together, these books report a revolution largely accomplished at home and a challenge still to be met abroad.

Bob Herbert hasn't written a book, but in his *New York Times* op-ed column of August 8, 2009, after a shooter had entered an aerobics class in a Pennsylvania gym to shoot women, he reiterated a question he had raised some years previously when Amish schoolgirls were singled out for shooting: Why is the shooting of women and girls not considered a hate crime? His suggestion was that we have yet "to acknowledge that misogyny is a serious and pervasive problem," not only in the developing world but right here at home. "There would have been thunderous outrage if someone had separated potential victims by race or religion and shot, say, only the blacks, or only the Jews." Life in the United States is, as he says, "mind-bogglingly violent," and yet there is a reluctance to "take particular notice of the staggering amounts of violence brought down on the nation's women and girls each and every day for no other reason than who they are. They are attacked because they are females."

"Lighten-up," a woman on CNN was told when she objected to the sale of Hillary nutcrackers, and the same advice was given in another 2009 *Times* op-ed, "The Mismeasure of Women," written by Joanne Lipman, a former deputy managing editor at *The Wall Street Journal*. "We were post-feminists," she writes. "After all, we lived equally with men. We felt that when we took our place in society, issues of gender—and race too—wouldn't be a factor." Yet she now sees that

> even the positive numbers we've heard about during the recession are misleading—the ones that seem to indicate that women have suffered fewer job losses then men. The reason? Women are still concentrated in lower-paying fields, rather than the high-paying industries like finance and real estate that were hardest hit.

In an astute observation, she connects the aftermath of the 9/11 attacks with a rise in misogyny: "I don't think it's a coincidence that exactly at this moment, women began losing ground—and not just in measureable ways, like how many women make partner or get jobs as chief executives. I'm referring here to how we're perceived." She doesn't explain the connection she makes, but the attacks of 9/11 were perceived by many as an insult to America and a humiliation of American manhood. This demanded a restoration of honor and a reassertion of dominance—of our ability to "shock and awe." And, as Lipman notes, it encouraged sexist attitudes and behavior (like the display of Hillary nutcrackers in airport shops). A friend who was teaching an MBA seminar at the time of the shock and awe bombings reported that among her students it was the women and the few European men present who spoke about the people being killed on the ground.

Searching the internet before a TV appearance for information on one of her interviewers, Lipman "got a full page of results about her breasts." Puzzling over this and similar evidence that we have lost our way, she comes to the realization that "part of the reason we've lost our way, part of the reason my generation has become complacent, is that many of us have been defining progress for women too narrowly. We've focused primarily on numbers at the expense of attitudes."

Reading along and nodding in agreement, I was unprepared for what followed. Having identified the problem as not "simply a women's issue" but one that affects us all, men and women alike, Lipman then urges women to "have a sense of humor." In short, lighten up.

There's much to be said for humor, especially when it breaks through denial; millions of Americans now rely for their news on Jon Stewart and The Colbert Report. But when humor is used to camouflage reality, it reinforces our penchant for turning away from what we know or making light of what we find discomforting.

III. Where are we going?

My friend Wendy Puriefoy, who heads the Public Education Network, likes to observe that there is a difference between saying to someone, "you can come into my house, you can come into any room of my house, but it's still my house," and saying, "let's redesign the house." She tells a story I hear as a parable. Years after the civil rights movement, after the Civil Rights and Voting Rights Acts were passed, an African-American died and went to heaven. St. Peter was waiting for him at the gate. "Boy," he said, to remind him of where he had come from, "What did you do with your freedom?"

It is my question for myself and other women—the question Virginia Woolf raises in *Three Guineas*, her essay on men and women and war. Writing on the eve of World War II, she links the hands of fascism and patriarchy, observing "that the public and the private worlds are inseparably connected; that the tyrannies and servilities of the one are the tyrannies and servilities of the other" (p. 168). At issue in both are what Josephine Butler called "the great principles of Justice and Equality and Liberty."

Composing her book as her long-delayed answer to a letter from a man asking, "How in your opinion are we to prevent war?" Woolf reframes the question to ask more pointedly: How can women help men to prevent war? (p. 5). The fight against tyranny joins women and men who aspire in common to justice, equality, and liberty. But to help men, women must first gain the freedom of an independent opinion supported by an independent income. Thus Woolf lays out a three-step progression for women: first to obtain a college education; second to enter the professions. Then, armed with an independent opinion and an independent income, to secure their freedom by forming a "Society of Outsiders." Rather than joining what Erikson called "the compact majority," those who live and play by the rules—or as Woolf puts it, rather than repeating men's words and following men's methods—women can use their freedom to help

61

men prevent war "by finding new words and creating new methods" (p. 170).

With record numbers of women now graduating from college and entering the professions, the question becomes: will they take up this challenge? Staying outside but joining with men in the pursuit of equality, liberty, and justice for all. What are the incentives for women to use their freedom to do creative work?

There are no simple answers to these questions, but there is a guide. Hrdy's work in evolutionary anthropology highlights the importance of empathy, mind-reading, and collaboration. She reminds us that "flexibility was, and continues to be, the hallmark of the human family" (p. 164). Neuroscientists (Antonio Damasio, Joseph LeDoux) tell us that in the absence of trauma or injury our nervous systems are hard-wired to connect emotion and thought. In our bodies and our emotions, we register our experience. The psyche follows an associative pattern that is idiosyncratic: your associations to the word "mother" may differ from mine and diverge from cultural scripts about mothers and mothering. Within ourselves, we harbor the seeds of creative work. And if women bring their so-called feminine (i.e. human) perceptions and inclinations into the workplace, the form of the workplace will change. The lesson of studies of airplane accidents and medical errors is that collaborative groups are more effective in averting tragedies because everyone feels free to speak up. What if this became a model for the law, the education system, and the church?

This takes me back to the research with girls. To recapitulate briefly, by following girls through middle childhood and well into adolescence, my colleagues and I saw evidence of resistance to those separations that are socially scripted and enforced. This resistance is manifest in an honest voice, reflecting our ability to pick up and register the feeling of what happens and the desire for relationship or mutual understanding. Because it is resisting, it is not necessarily a nice voice, a voice that other people want to hear. It is a voice that can make trouble in families, schools, and communities. Consequently, it is a voice that girls begin to cover. It is easier, sixteen-year-old Sheila tells me, to say "I don't like myself enough to look out for myself" than for her to reveal how she looks out for herself: by never saying what she really feels and thinks. "Brilliant, isn't it?" she asks, looking at me, and I agree. Whatever people may say about her, it doesn't really affect her because they don't know who she is. But however brilliant this is as a strategy for self-protection, it is at the expense of what Sheila said she most wanted: "honesty in relationships."

At the crossroads of adolescence, girls may bury an honest voice inside themselves for safe-keeping in the face of pressures to cave in and commit what Woolf calls "adultery of the brain," by which she means betraying your mind. I remember noticing in our interview transcripts that girls were flagging the onset of adolescence with a sharp rise in their use of the phrase "I don't know," often coupled with an increase in the phrase, "you know." At first it made sense that in entering a new terrain, girls would be struck by what in fact they did not know. And "you know" is such a conversational tic among adolescent girls that I found it annoying rather than of interest. But as I began to question what girls seemed not to know, given what they had known previously, I came to a new understanding. In the phrase "I don't know," the word "don't" jumped out as an injunction standing between "I" and "know." Whose word was that? Parents? Teachers? Preachers? Or something in the air that girls pick up? Wherever it came from, it resided inside, becoming an inner voice mandating dissociation: don't say this, don't think this, don't feel this. In short, don't know what you know; ignore the promptings of your body and your emotions. Listen instead to the voices that tell you what is happening and what you should feel and think and say. Don't listen to yourself.

The longitudinal span of our interview data caught girls moving from knowing to not knowing and also their resistance to losing what we can now recognize not as women's intuition but as basic human capacities—the capacities Hrdy describes. Girls are caught between their ability to read other minds and a culture that tells us we can't read other minds, between their empathy and desire for connection and a society that places a premium on separateness and independence, between an impulse to work cooperatively and the rewards to be gained by working competitively. "I don't know," "you know," along with the repetitive tap "I mean," conveyed a struggle around knowing and a search to find words for experiences that elude our vocabulary.

Judy, as a philosophical nine-year-old, explains that the mind is where you feel things. "I just feel it in my mind," she says, referring to how she knows how her best friend feels when someone walks away from her. "You can kind of just see them walking away or getting sad or

64

something, but you can't tell right then and there she's going to get hurt or anything, but you just feel it. It's hard to explain." The interviewer notes that what Judy seems to be saying is that while she doesn't consciously think "my friend is going to be hurt," she senses and feels her friend's sadness and thus knows it. As Spinoza observed, the mind is the body in thought. Judy's mind knows what she feels in her body, and her body picks up the feelings of others, which resonate in her mind.

At thirteen, Judy reads the human world around her with psychological acuity, observing that the fight at the dinner table that broke out over her eight-year-old sister's refusal to eat the carrots "was not about the carrots." She also reads the culture in which she is coming of age, its splitting of intellect from emotion, mind from body, self from relationships. Facing the quandary of how to reconcile what she knows with what is considered to be knowledge, Judy arrives at a creative solution. She splits her mind not from her body but from her brain, which she locates in her head and associates with her intelligence, her smartness, and her education. Speaking of her mind, she points to her gut and explains:

> A mind has your real thoughts and a brain sort of has the intelligence . . . what you learn in school . . . physics and statistics and all that, but your mind is associated with your heart and your soul and your internal feeling and your real feelings.

People, she says,

> can control what they're teaching you and say, "This is right and this is wrong." That's control like into your

brain. But the feeling is just with you. The feeling can't be changed by someone else who wants it to be this way. It can't be changed by saying, "No this is wrong, this is right, this is wrong."

As the interview draws to a close, Judy states her theory of development:

I think that maybe really young children have . . . [mind] more than anyone else because I don't know, they don't have much of a brain . . . and I think that's when you get all your mind stuff because that's the only thing you really have then, because then you . . . transform some of the mind things to the brain, so then that starts to evolve and that's sort of like the way you are brought up. It goes into your brain. And I think that after a while, you just sort of forget your mind, because everything is being shoved at you into your brain.

Judy is thirteen, a reflective eighth-grader, struggling with dissociation and arriving at a creative solution for holding onto what she knows. She contends with a voice that carries the force of moral authority and would lead her to forget her mind, a voice she experiences as intrusive and controlling. You can forget your mind, she says, but the "deeper sort of knowing," the knowing she associates with her heart and her soul and her real thoughts and feelings, can't be changed by someone saying, "No, this is wrong, this is right." However forceful the initiation, however linked with smartness, intelligence, and education and all they imply, the "feeling is just with you," a gut knowing, buried perhaps but not lost.

Judy's concern that children are losing their minds

finds an echo in Hrdy's concern that we are losing our capacity for mutual understanding:

> If empathy and understanding develop only under particular rearing conditions, and if an ever-increasing proportion of the species fails to encounter these conditions but nevertheless survives to reproduce, it won't matter how valuable the underpinnings for collaboration were in the past. Compassion and the quest for emotional connection will fade away as surely as sight in cave-dwelling fish. (p. 293)

The establishment of hierarchy relies on dissociation to sever connections that stand in its way. Mutual understanding is horizontal in structure, inherently democratic. To turn the horizontal into a vertical with higher and lower, good and bad, a series of splits are essential. If the capacity for mutual understanding—for empathy, mind-reading, and cooperation—is innate, this capacity has to be broken or at the very least relegated to the margins. This is the task of patriarchal initiation, which if successful implants in the psyche things foreign to our human nature. Resilient girls such as Judy will resist the pressures they feel to split their minds from their bodies, their thoughts from their emotions, themselves from their relationships. Pressures to bury an honest voice, which in our post-modern culture is said not to exist. In such a context, it becomes hard for girls like Judy to know what they know without feeling crazy. And saying what they know, especially what they know about the people around them, can make trouble for others and for themselves.

At thirteen, Judy can't talk about the troubles in her

family. "I'd feel really bad," she says when her interviewer asks her if there is any way she could speak about these things. "I know what you're asking, but I don't know. I'm trying to think." Her thinking is impeded by dissociative processes. She reflects that were she an outsider looking in, she would probably think they should just talk about it, but she says, "That's not even on my list." "Why?" the interviewer persists:

> I don't know, because I don't—I don't know. I mean, I do know. It's just like—I can't explain—I don't know what, how to put it into words . . . I don't even know if I know what it is. So I can't really explain it. Because I don't know. I don't even know like in my brain or in my heart what I am really feeling. I mean I don't know if it's pain or upsetness or sad—I don't know.

Were she an outsider, she would talk about what's going on in her family, but being inside it, she can't know or explain what she knows without "feel[ing] really bad."

At New York University, I teach a seminar on listening, for doctoral students doing psychological research. Each year, I begin with the observation that research starts with a question. And each year I discover that the doctoral students have a hard time asking a real question. Having risen to the pinnacle of the educational system, they have no trouble asking "good questions." They know the right questions, the ones they should ask. But in my class where I teach a method of research geared to psychological discovery, they are called upon to ask a real question, meaning simply a question that is real for them. Something they want to know but don't know. Something that would lead them, as the course requires, to engage with another person in an effort to discover what they, my students, want to know.

When they first formulate their real question, rooting it both in their lives and in their field, what they know about their question is transparent, at the surface of their consciousness. What they don't know but want to know is barely audible. I ask them to draw a line down a page and on one side write what they know about their question and on the other what they don't know but want to know. Still they have trouble, which surfaces then in the interviews they conduct when they find themselves without a rudder—not knowing which way to steer. Your question is your rudder, I tell them, and curiosity the motor to propel you forward when the wind dies down. Still they get lost.

They transcribe their interviews and begin a series of guided listenings that direct their ear to the psychological logic of the interview conversation, not evident on the surface of the text. First they listen for the plot—the psychological landscape (the stories told, ruptures and gaps, emotional hot spots, their own responses). Then they listen for the "I," following the first-person voice of their interviewee in its associative stream and composing an "I poem" (for example, in the last quotation from Judy, the I poem would read: "I don't know, I don't, I don't know, / I mean, I do know, / I can't, I don't know, I don't even know, / I know, / I can't, I don't know, I don't, / I am, I mean, / I don't know, I don't know"—the stanza breaks marking psychic cadences, like the places where a singer might pause for breath). Finally, they listen for the different voices in the text that speak to their question—such as the voice of knowing and the voice of not knowing, or the voice of resistance and the voice of capitulation—and track their interplay or counterpoint. When they are then asked to assemble the evidence they have gathered from these listenings, something transformative frequently happens.

At this point in my class, in the fall of 2009, everyone cried; not a crying that signaled distress but a quiet rain of tears, expressing the release they felt in finally breaking through. Despite all my efforts, their questions had remained dissociated from a knowing that resided inside themselves. They were students, after all, and this was a class, not therapy. What was called for was objectivity not subjectivity, research not mesearch. Yet their interviewees' responses to their question had surprised them. From listening to another human being, what they learned, both about themselves and the interviewee, had the ring of genuine discovery. Tracking the associative logic of psychological processes, they were undoing dissociations within themselves. In Judy's terms, they were joining their intelligence, honed through their education, with a deeper sort of knowing that felt transgressive in crossing the boundaries between subject and object, intellect and emotion. Yet they were coming to original insights and doing creative work.

I was struck by a gender difference that surfaced at this juncture. The discussion that led this particular session to become "such a great class," as one woman commented, had been initiated by Dan, the only man in the group aside from the teaching assistant. Along with several others that week, Dan had not turned in his assignment. He said he had found it "overwhelming." So many thoughts rushed through his mind that he found himself unable to assemble them, and the rise of emotion led him to fear that if he continued, he would "break down." A woman faced with a similar experience who also did not turn in her assignment had rented a car over the weekend and driven to Vermont, playing the tape of her interview over and over on the car stereo and watching the leaves as she followed the thoughts and feelings evoked by what she was hearing. Dan's response to the rise in his feelings was to say "no, no, no, no" and "scurry away," just as he had done at the point in the interview when, in responding to his question about the American dream, Rose, his interviewee, began to speak of her struggle with infertility. This had taken him by surprise even though his question had roots in his own strong feelings about the fact that as a gay man he couldn't have children, at least not in the usual way, and thus, in his eyes, could not realize the American dream of having a family.

Dan looked around, clearly at sea. Seeking to reassure him, Melanie said that although she had turned in her paper, it was not her best work. Which startled me, because in fact it was. It was the first work of hers I found interesting; in part because, as she wrote in her paper, she had found "a nugget of gold" in an interview that up to that point had seemed rather boring. The nugget of gold was an insight into her question, which had to do with people's responses or lack of response to the environmental crisis. When I read the excerpt of her paper aloud, Melanie blushed, a smile opening her face. What she had said to reassure Dan was not in fact what she really thought and felt. This was the opening the other women walked through, one after one. They would say what they really felt and thought, often with tears.

"I have no problem with crying," Anna said, repeating what I had said some weeks earlier when a student became tearful in expressing her relief at learning a method that encouraged rather than discouraged her from pursuing her own questions. "Do any of you have a problem with crying?" Anna asked the class, again following my example. Everyone said no, they had no problem with this expression of emotion in the middle of the morning. I noted that the class had formed a culture of its own.

In his responses to her question about his experience of graduate education, Anna had distinguished three voices in her interviewee, Micah: a "locked-in" voice that conveyed his frustrations with his graduate program; an "honest" voice that interrupted it, always prefaced by the phrase "to be honest"; and a "revisionist-his-story" voice in which Micah reframed his story. In her final paper for the class, Anna wrote: "In this voice, [Micah] offers up new narrative about his place in graduate school, his roles as a teacher, and his current close relationship with his mother (a professor)." In the real time of the interview, Micah had come to a new understanding of why he had chosen to pursue a doctorate in the humanities rather than going to law school as he had planned. What initially had felt like something of a trap became, in his words, "a joyful obligation."

"It changed my life," Anna said beaming, tears

running down her face. She shared with Micah an African-American heritage; they both were outstanding students with many options to choose from. After college, Anna had worked to help students of color gain access to elite universities, and her question (how do students of color experience graduate education) was rooted in this experience. She had assumed she would learn something from Micah's responses, but she had not anticipated the resonant chord his three voices struck within herself. Taking down the protective wall she had built between her African-American culture with its values and the university culture in which she excelled, she told the class of mostly white students that she now knew why she wanted to stay in graduate school, why she wanted a Ph.D. in education. I recall the beauty of Anna's face that day when she dropped her guard. When she turned in her final paper, I noticed that her writing had become more fluent, more accessible.

Erika's interview with TJ—a tall, broad-shouldered eighteen-year-old with his hair in cornrows and a tattoo wreathing his arm—also touched off a resonance she had not expected. She had rooted her question—how do teenage boys experience abortion?—in her years of experience leading a theater troupe for adolescent girls, several of whom had had abortions, and in the literature on boys' psychology. Nothing prepared her for TJ's emotional candor, his access to his feelings about both the pregnancy and the abortion, his empathy, his intuitive knowing that led him to pick up on his girlfriend's pregnancy before she told him, his emotional connection with the child they conceived and also with his mother, and his ability to stay emotionally present with his girl-friend through the entire experience. But Erika was also taken aback by the realization that her question was rooted in a decision she had made some years previously when she decided not to tell her boyfriend she was pregnant. Erika's interview with TJ challenged widely held assumptions about teenage boys, at the same time as it led her to see, more pointedly, that in holding these assumptions herself, she had overlooked what she knew about her boyfriend. As she wrote in her paper, she knew him to be a caring and compassionate man.

My teaching assistant, an advanced doctoral student, had responded to Dan's difficulty in completing his assignment by recalling that when he had taken the class some years previously, he too had found it difficult to stay present in the face of strong emotions. As the session drew to a close, he worried that Dan might have heard what he said as "critical," which Dan hadn't, nor had anyone else in the class. My teaching assistant then reflected that this session of the class had been "difficult" and "upsetting"—seeking to acknowledge what he had taken to be the students' experience. I noted that the words "difficult" and "upsetting" had not been used by any of the women. They too had found the assignment challenging, but they had spoken not of breaking down but of breaking through. The wall seemed more permeable for them, and in breaking through it, they provided a resonance, encouraging Dan to break through as well. By the end of the session, his eyes were moist and his face had opened, perhaps in response to the women's demonstration that it was possible to break through without breaking down.

IV. Why should we still study gender?

It is by now a common perception, at least among those involved in primary education, that boys' resilience is at heightened risk in the transition from early to middle childhood. One has only to think of the frequency with which Ritalin is prescribed for boys at this time. Their problems are usually ascribed to neurological disorders and to the way primary schools are set up. Whatever the explanation, the longstanding observation holds: boys show more signs of psychological distress in what Freud called the Oedipal period while girls experience a similarly heightened risk to their resilience at the time of adolescence. This difference has been noticed over and over again but never explained in any way that accounted for the hardiness of girls during early and middle childhood beyond the fact that they are not boys. In his *New Introductory Lectures*, Freud recorded his impression that "little girls are more intelligent and livelier than boys of the same age; they go out more to meet the external world and at the same time form stronger object-cathexes [i.e., relationships]" (p. 146), but then he dismissed this difference as not of great consequence. In talking about the higher incidence of depression among young boys as well as the rash of learning and attention disorders, speech and behavior problems, people—experts, parents, journalists—speak about the nervous system, developmental lags in boys, the structure of schooling, and the greater fragility of male infants. No one has spoken about initiation.

The research on girls' development, in solving the "riddle of femininity," elucidated a process of initiation that mandates dissociation and in effect drives a stake through the psyche. The riddle of femininity is in fact the riddle of femininity in patriarchy, which forces girls to choose between having a voice and having relationships. Girls' resistance to making a choice they recognize as psychologically incoherent, whether consciously or by registering the incoherence in their bodies and their emotions, leads them to be described as having a problem with separation. Which they do. They are having a problem separating their minds from their bodies, their thoughts from their emotions, their honest voices from their relationships: separations that entail a sacrifice of both voice and relationship and lead them to lose touch with what they know and who they are.

The man-as-hunter hypothesis of anthropology and socio-biology continues to drive the culture wars, and the Cartesian split still reigns in university classrooms, just as the Oedipal family remains enshrined in psychoanalysis. These mainstays of patriarchy have all been contested. Recording his journey into the heart of darkness, Sven Lindqvist, a Swedish journalist, begins and ends by speaking of dissociation: "You already know enough. So do I. It is not knowledge we lack. What is missing is the courage to understand what we know and to draw conclusions" (*Exterminate All the Brutes*, p. 2).

Until we address the problem of false memory—both in feminism and within ourselves—the divisions among women will continue, as will the argument as to whether women are different from or the same as men, and if different, who is better. Until we locate the origins of these gender binaries and hierarchies in patriarchy and recognize misogyny as a hate crime, we will not understand why freedom remains so elusive and love so threatening. Child care, health care, and the care of our planet will baffle us. We won't understand why we can't end poverty and stop war. Gender is at the root of these problems, and, at least for now, we need to study it.

In the fable of the Feminist in the pro-seminar, the quotation posted in the elevator read: "Speak what you feel, not what you ought to say." In Shakespeare's play, the pronoun is "we." We have traversed an historical era during which the referent of feminism shifted from a we that meant women to one that means human, a shift echoed in the human sciences. We have also witnessed the expansion of the feminist vision from liberating women to freeing everyone by liberating democracy from patriarchy. I return then to the line at the end of *King Lear* to restore the we and quote the final quatrain. It encompasses the moral of the fable, the theme of this chapter, and also Sarah Hrdy's uncertainty as to whether our descendants "will still be human in ways that we now think of as distinguishing our species—that is, empathic and curious about the emotions of others, shaped by our ancient heritage of communal care" (p. 294).

> The weight of this sad time we must obey;
> Speak what we feel, not what we ought to say.
> The oldest have borne most; we that are young
> Shall never see so much, nor live so long.

3 Free Association and the Grand Inquisitor: A Psychoanalytic Drama

Like a play, this chapter is driven by dramatic tension. The Setting: psychoanalysis. The Time: more than a century, continuing to the present. The Place: Vienna and the U.S.

You will recognize most of the characters—Freud certainly, the Grand Inquisitor perhaps—and also many of the events, but the story I tell reflects a discovery that took me by surprise. I came to see a familiar history in a new light, reflecting a tension within psychoanalysis that mirrors a tension in the history of liberal democracy and also, perhaps, within ourselves.

You may need to know a few things about me that you will not find on Google but which are relevant to the drama I unfold. I have a long and enduring relationship with psychoanalysis, dating from that summer when my mother took me, aged two, to Clara Thompson's institute at Vassar. There I discovered the power of voice and resistance. This relationship picked up again when I was in graduate school and Freud became my salvation from despair. I was studying clinical psychology with the intention of becoming a therapist, but having spent my undergraduate years immersed in Shakespeare and Tolstoy, Joyce, Faulkner and Woolf, I was taken aback by the readings we were assigned: journal articles and clinical cases where the banality of the descriptions of people and their lives was covered by an array of numbers, cloaked in what passed for objectivity, and conveyed in a voice of expertise that veiled an attitude of superiority if not contempt. I took to my bed, and, playing my recording of Handel's *Messiah* over and over to the exasperation of the other graduate students on my hall, spent my days reading Freud along with Chekhov and Ibsen, and at night went out with my boyfriend.

A solution to the problem of graduate school appeared early in my second year when I fell in love with Jim Gilligan, and on a snowy night in Cambridge, we conceived a child. A messiah had appeared, saving me from my endless obsession over whether to go back to the study of literature, which had been my undergraduate major, or go to medical school as my mother's friend Sophie advised. Instead, Jim and I went to Cleveland where he went to medical school and I was free to hang out with our newborn son Jonathan, supported by a grant to finish my dissertation. I had grown up with a playful grandfather, and days spent in play recalled some of the happiest memories of my childhood. Sitting with Jonathan on the floor, playing with blocks and small cars, was a welcome respite from graduate training, which my friend, the late psychologist Bernie Kaplan, compared to "dressage." I wrote one of the shortest dissertations on record, titled "Responses to Temptation:

an analysis of motives," and with a new clarity as to my own desires and values, took my two-year-old with me to register voters in Cleveland's African-American community where I also joined, at Karamu House, their lively arts center, a performing modern dance company.

Having discovered the joys of making love not war, I became another mother for peace. When Jim interned at the University of Chicago and I used my newly minted Harvard Ph.D. to earn a little money by teaching very part-time in the college, my activism led to a brief encounter with the ways psychoanalysis can be used to quell political protest. I was among the mostly junior faculty who refused to submit our grades once they began to be used as a basis for deciding who would go to Vietnam, and I must have been something of a ring-leader in that protest because I was summoned by the provost, a lawyer who as it turned out was a friend of a friend of my father. In the chilly formality of his forbidding office, he dismissed my impassioned act of resistance by interpreting my ethical objections as a sign of my rebellion against my father.

Rebellion was certainly in the air: The Winter Soldiers Movement (the anti-Vietnam War protest that began within the military) was followed by the Summer of Love, and many walls were tumbling down. It is difficult now to recapture the sudden sense of freedom and all the challenges it posed. I remember the thrill of the March on Washington, the civil rights legislation that followed, and even now the songs of the Beatles bring back the light-hearted humor that was in the air, along with the passion for justice.

Jim and I returned to Harvard, he to do his psychiatric

residency, I to care for our now three sons. There I had
the opportunity to teach with Erik Erikson in his course
on the human life cycle. Again I was reading Freud,
but now also finding in Erikson a mentor, a person
who joined psychology with history, clinical work with
an artist's sensibility, inspiring me and showing me a
way. However, when Jim finished his psychiatric residency and entered the Boston Psychoanalytic Institute,
becoming a candidate and beginning his own analysis,
I encountered the mentality I remembered from my
summer at Vassar. Again a wall was erected, this time
within our marriage. Jim's analyst told him that for the
sake of the analysis, he was not to discuss his analysis
with me. I will not go into all that followed from this
breach in our custom of talking about everything. Suffice
it to say that Jim eventually left the Institute to pursue
his passion, turning his psychoanalytically trained ear to
the study of violence, and I wrote *In a Different Voice*,
largely for myself, in response to a voice welling up
inside me saying, 'If you want to know what I think—,'
but secure in the conviction that aside from myself and
my family and friends, no one really was interested.

I began my own analysis after my book was published, at a time when I was involved in what became
for me the most radically illuminating research. Having
discovered that women's psychology, including the
feminist psychology of that time, was divorced from
its foundation in girls' development, having learned
from Joseph Adelson's 1980 *Handbook of Adolescent
Psychology* that the psychology of adolescence was "the
study of the male youngster writ large," and having
observed that of all the voices in *In a Different Voice*,

81

the one women readers found most arresting, was that of eleven-year-old Amy, I set out to fill in a missing stretch of psychological history. I would chart the coming-of-age experience from the vantage point not of boys but of girls.

So it happened that as I, in my analysis, was going back through my own life history, I was also listening to girls going forward from childhood into adolescence. What took me by surprise was the Proustian experience of remembering what had been a lost time. Like the taste of a madeleine dipped in tea, girls' voices at the edge of adolescence opened a vast storehouse of recollection. Through free association and with the help of my analyst, I was undoing dissociations within myself at the same time as I was witnessing the onset of dissociative processes in the girls I was studying, literally hearing them narrate their moves into not knowing as the injunction "don't" came between "I" and "know." In this way, I discovered the extent to which I and other women, heeding this injunction, had rewritten our own life histories to conform with accepted scripts. And I realized that, with the notable exception of artists, this rewritten history, culturally encouraged and sanctioned by psychologists, was commonly mistaken for truth. Culture was being misread as nature, and a process of initiation interpreted as a stage in human development. Separations that served to perpetuate divisions among women and between women and men, along with the privileging of masculine qualities, were taken as the "natural" order of things. All of this was sustained by dissociation and manifest in a loss of voice and memory.

My analysis in the hands of my free-thinking analyst

released me at a deeper level from ways of thinking so firmly entrenched that they were readily taken for how things are rather than how things are said to be. *In a Different Voice* was a beginning, but without my analysis and my ongoing relationship with Jim, I might not have built the courage I needed to risk the work that eventually followed. The twenty-year journey from *In a Different Voice* to *The Birth of Pleasure* had been devoted to research connecting women's psychology with girls' development, followed by a study of young boys and an exploration of impasses in love between women and men. All of this work was collaborative, and I wrote five books with my students (*Meeting at the Crossroads* and *Between Voice and Silence*, along with three edited volumes). But in *The Birth of Pleasure*, I set out on my own to take on what I saw as a persisting dissociation, keeping research on girls apart from the mainland of human understanding. For example, although *Meeting at the Crossroads: Women's Psychology and Girls' Development*, written with Lyn Mikel Brown, was hailed as a *New York Times* notable book of the year, reviews in *The New Republic* and *The Nation* ran under the headline "Gilligan's Island."

I had been following an associative stream, picking up resonances between the voices of children in contemporary American settings and voices recorded by artists across time and cultures (from Iphigenia in Euripides' tragedy and Viola in Shakespeare's *Twelfth Night* to Tambu in Tsi Tsi Dangarembga's *Nervous Conditions* and Claudia in Toni Morrison's *The Bluest Eye*). I had been struck by the resemblance between the onset of dissociative processes in young boys and a forgetting

I witnessed among men and the recollections of early childhood Proust's narrator comes to in *In Search of Lost Time*. When I learned from Denise DeCosta, a young Dutch scholar, that Anne Frank had edited her diary and that most of both the actual diary and her edited version had been saved and were published in the 1989 *Critical Edition* of the diary, I realized that a process of self-editing that I knew within myself and had observed in my studies with girls and women had been caught by the net of history, preserved like a fossil in amber.

I wrote *The Birth of Pleasure* in an associative voice, linking myths with my own dreams, research with my own memories as well as with literature and legends, to show that within ourselves we know a path of resistance leading to love and freedom. And although we may not know that we know this path, it is part of our cultural heritage, preserved in Apuleius' telling of the myth of Psyche and Cupid (or Eros), carried forward in the plays of Shakespeare (who borrowed extensively from Apuleius), as well as in novels and folktales, including the "women-centered tales" from India collected by Professor A. K. Ramanujan.

As an undergraduate at Swarthmore, I had taken seminars on perception with Hans Wallach, a leading Gestalt psychologist. I was fascinated by the demonstrations of illusion (how the moon looks larger on the horizon than at the zenith, how stationary lights can appear to be moving) and also by our ability to see through illusion, as when the rotation of a square on a screen reveals the edge and we recognize that it is a cube. Freud, among others, had noted that artists are often far ahead in their perceptions—in part, I thought, because they rely on associative methods that elude the cultural radar. Just as you can't argue yourself out of dissociation (as the song goes, "you don't know what you don't know"), so in dismantling a framework that in upholding patriarchal norms and values was pseudo-science not science, I could not work within the structure of that framework. In Woolf's terms, I needed to find new words and create new methods.

I wrote a novel, *Kyra*, having surprised myself during my analysis by starting to write fiction. And as I worked with my son Jonathan to turn our play "The Scarlet Letter" into a libretto for "Pearl," an opera, I also worked with my NYU colleague David Richards on *The Deepening Darkness*, integrating my studies of psychological development with David's studies of ethical resistance to expose the roots of an ethically resisting voice grounded not in ideology but in what is now recognized as our human nature.

Thus I come to the drama of this chapter, a tension in method and theory that runs through the history of psychoanalysis, and to the question implied by its title: whether, as Dostoevsky's parable of the Grand Inquisitor and Erich Fromm's book (*Escape From Freedom*) suggest, our desire for freedom is countered not only from without but also from within by a desire to escape from freedom. I will draw on material from *The Deepening Darkness*, and where I use the pronoun "we," I am referring to David Richards and myself. Our subtitle, *Patriarchy, Resistance, and Democracy's Future*, sums up our thesis: democracy's future hinges on resistance to patriarchy, but our title is indebted to

Freud, who observed in a letter to Lou Andreas-Salomé that he needed to deepen the darkness in order to see what has faint light to it. As we embarked on our study of patriarchal institutions and practices with an eye to discerning the shoots of ethical resistance, we came to a startling observation. Across time and cultures, from the Rome of Augustus to the 1960s, an ethically resisting voice, meaning a voice that resists injustice, was accompanied by a sexually resisting voice, a voice that resists patriarchal Love Laws—Arundhati Roy's term for the laws that establish "who should be loved. And how. And how much." This link with sexuality takes us to Freud; and so, without further ado . . .

ACT I
The time is 1895, the characters are Freud and Breuer, coauthors of *Studies on Hysteria*, along with The Women who had become hysterical.

Psyche, the young woman who was forbidden to see or to say what she knew about love, is stage center in *Studies on Hysteria*. In a rush of discovery, Breuer and Freud lay bare the profound connection between our minds and our bodies by tracing the conversion of psychic pain into physical pain. They describe the process of dissociation, the splitting of consciousness so that parts of our experience lie outside our awareness. And in their treatment of hysterical young women, they discover the power of association to undo dissociation, unlocking secrets held in the psyche. It is the psychological equivalent to discovering fire.

Like Psyche, the women in *Studies on Hysteria* were not only victims but also resisters; at one and the same time they internalized the taboo against speaking while communicating symbolically with their bodies, their symptoms. Freud's key, his "pick-lock," was to reverse the process underlying the hysteria. Observing that hysterics suffer mainly from reminiscences, he moved their memories out of their bodies and into language.

When the "lost" or silenced voice of hysteria was found, however, all hell broke loose—to summon the image from the *Aeneid* that Freud would choose as the epigraph for his *Interpretation of Dreams*: *Flectere si nequero superbo Acheronta movebo* (If I cannot move the upper world, I will move the underworld). He had not been able to move the upper world—his colleagues in medicine and in the university—with the insights of his studies on hysteria. So now he would appeal to the underworld, to dreams, finding in his own dreams the royal road to the unconscious. The path he took is marked by quotations from the *Aeneid* that appear in his writings at just this juncture: *Forsan et haec olim meminisse juvebit*—Some day, perhaps, it will be a joy to remember even these things ("Screen Memories" [1899]); *Exoriare aliquis nostris ex ossibus ulto*—May someone arise from my bones, an avenger ("The Forgetting of Foreign Words" [1901]); and the just-quoted epigraph for *The Interpretation of Dreams*. They flag an identification with Aeneas that provides us with a clue to what follows. As Aeneas left Dido and Carthage to found Rome, so Freud will leave the hysterics and the insights he gained from working with them to found the institution of psychoanalysis.

We see how quickly the discoveries of the *Studies on Hysteria* became burdened with radical implications.

Freud referred to his early women patients as his teachers, and what they taught him gave him insight not only into the workings of the psyche but also into the connections between inner and outer worlds, the psyche and the culture in which it is embedded. In *Studies on Hysteria*, the knowing carried symbolically by hysterical symptoms resembles what has now come to be recognized as the "implicit relational knowing of the human infant" (the immediate visceral knowing that leads babies, for example, to scream when picked up by someone who is out of touch). In the early, heady days of psychoanalysis, the knowing expressed indirectly through symptoms became the explicit relational knowing of young women and also of their physicians.

In Tennessee Williams' play *A Streetcar Named Desire*, when Blanche is raped by her sister Stella's husband Stanley, she tells Stella what has happened. Stella then tells her friend Eunice, "I couldn't believe her story and go on living with Stanley." The insight of this realization illuminates the history of psychoanalysis: Freud could not believe the incest stories of his women patients and go on living in patriarchy. But the issue from our perspective is even more pointed. The discoveries of the *Studies on Hysteria* had led Freud to see trauma and specifically the traumatizing of sexuality as the *caput Nili*, the head of the Nile, the source of neurotic suffering. This is an insight that Sandor Ferenczi and Ian Suttie would also come to, but they read the trauma more broadly as the traumatizing of voice and thus of relationship. The traumatized person, experiencing his or her own voice as ineffective, as powerless, adopts the voice that carries power and authority. Stella cannot take on Blanche's voice and all it implies within a culture where Stanley holds the power. Or rather, to take on Blanche's voice would mean protesting the culture on ethical grounds.

It was the separation of women from their own stories that initially caught Breuer and Freud's attention. "Her love had already been separated from her knowledge," Freud writes of the woman he calls Fraulein Elisabeth von R. By connecting women's love with their knowledge, Freud became a virtual Eve, or more accurately, the serpent in the garden. He was breaking a cultural taboo, undoing a process of initiation by forging a method of inquiry that placed him in direct opposition to the fundamental rule of patriarchy: the claim on the part of fathers to authority.

At the beginning, Freud suspected that Elisabeth's knowledge was a secret she was keeping from him, but he quickly discovered that she was also keeping the secret from herself. He had come upon dissociation, the splitting of consciousness through which we can come not to know what we know. Gaps in memory, broken trains of thought, something missing in a causal chain— these were the clues that alerted him to this silence. In a bold move, he decided to proceed on the assumption that "my patients knew everything that was of any pathogenic significance" with respect to their symptoms (*Studies on Hysteria*, p. 110). At moments when Elisabeth would break off her train of associations or claim that nothing was occurring to her, Freud, observing her tense and preoccupied expression, would touch her forehead and suggest that in fact she knew. Noting that his method never failed, he observed that the split-off knowledge was at once familiar and surprising. "I knew it," Elisabeth said, "I could have told you the first time." And yet she hadn't. It had taken both free association and a human touch to reconnect her with what she knew.

Freud was using his psychoanalytic method to unlock one of the deep secrets of patriarchy: what daughters know about their fathers, including the secret of father–daughter incest. Trauma, seen by Pierre Janet and other psychiatrists to be the bedrock of hysteria, becomes in Freud's understanding a sexual trauma, leading the psyche to dissociate from the body, which then becomes the repository of experiences that reside outside of consciousness. As Freud discovered the power of association—the stream of consciousness and the touch of relationship—to undo dissociation, the psyche opened to his investigation.

The challenge he faced in his early work lay in relinquishing the voice of the father. As a physician, he had claim to authority, yet his method depended on giving up that claim. His power lay in knowing a way—a method for freeing association. But only the patient knew the source of her suffering. By encouraging Elisabeth to know what she knew in her body and connect her voice with her experience, Freud was systematically (and paradoxically) undoing a process of initiation that had led her to take on a father's voice as her own. As her "frozen nature" began to melt, the pains in her legs subsided.

The psychology of trauma and the psychology of patriarchy converge at this juncture. The "confusion of tongues" that Ferenczi identifies as a telltale sign of trauma, the adoption of the aggressor's voice as one's own, becomes an identification with the father that marks the psyche's induction into a patriarchal order. But the identification is not necessarily with the father *per se*. Rather it is an identification with the voice of patriarchal authority, the law of the father, and the internalization of its demands. A process that appears adaptive thus contains a silence at its center, and in that silence we hear the loss of voice and the confusion of memory that make it difficult or impossible to say or even to know what actually happened. Freud's discovery of the power of association to undo dissociation gave him an entry into a cultural blind spot. His dream of aligning his new science with enlightenment and freedom was within his grasp.

ACT II

The year is 1899/1900. Freud enters carrying *The Interpretation of Dreams.*

According to the myth, Oedipus's father Laius had sexually abused a young boy. The god Apollo tells Laius that retribution will come in the next generation, at the hands of a son of his own. When Jocasta, Laius's wife, gives birth to a son, Laius enlists her in his plan to protect himself by killing the child. They drive a stake through his feet (hence the name Oedipus, which means swollen foot) and prepare to leave him on a hillside to die. Jocasta gives the baby to a shepherd to carry out the plan—or perhaps to subvert it, which the shepherd does, setting the plot in motion by giving Oedipus to another shepherd who takes him to Corinth to be raised there by the king and queen as their son.

91

As Oedipus grows up, the only sign of the trauma is the telltale mark on his feet. There is no voice speaking about what happened; he has no memory. When Oedipus learns that he is fated to kill his father and marry his mother, he leaves Corinth in an effort to avert his fate. At a crossroads, he kills an older man who confronted him in a fight over the right of way and then goes to Thebes where he solves the riddle of the Sphinx and marries the queen, an older woman.

In formulating the Oedipus Complex, Freud separates the wishes for incest and murder from the trauma story in which they are embedded. He casts them instead as universal fantasies, arising from inborn drives or instincts that play out in the triangle of father, mother, and child. The wishes to marry one's mother and kill one's father are countered by civilization, with its prohibitions on incest and murder. And the resulting dynamic of conflicting wishes and prohibitions (e.g. both desiring and hating one's mother, loving and wanting to kill one's father) form the Oedipus Complex. Rather than trauma, these inner conflicts become the seedbed for neuroses. Thus the Oedipus Complex, shorn of trauma, becomes the cornerstone of psychoanalysis.

With this placement or displacement, an astonishing change enters Freud's writings. Women, formerly regarded by Freud as his teachers, are now described as secretive by nature and stunted by civilization. We see Freud arguing with his women patients—with Irma and with Dora—claiming to know better than they do the meaning of their symptoms. Freud now assumes the position of the knower, the interpreter of dreams. And fathers, the incestuous fathers revealed through the studies on hysteria, now become the arbiters of conscience, morality, and law.

How can we understand these changes in Freud that would set the direction for psychoanalysis for much of the twentieth century? By linking the resolution of the Oedipus Complex to the child's identification with the father and internalization of his voice or law, Freud has aligned psychoanalysis with patriarchy, its inherent misogyny and its equation of a father's voice with moral authority. But if we look more closely, we see psychoanalytic processes at work. Wishes are disguised, the repressed returns, and displacements conceal what is actually going on—the very processes Freud describes in *The Interpretation of Dreams*.

We notice that at the same time Freud questions the pervasiveness of incest, he places an incest story—the Oedipus story—at the center of psychoanalysis. In *The Interpretation of Dreams*, he shifts his attention away from women's experiences of sexual trauma to his own fantasies of an incestuous relationship with his mother, fantasies that involve parricide as well. As he finds in his dreams the same themes that he sees in the great tragedies of Sophocles and Shakespeare, he aligns himself with civilization and retreats from the psychically intimate and fruitful relationships he had established with his women patients. The rush of discovery he experienced in these relationships and the deep human sympathy he felt with the women had become associated with danger and vulnerability, with the risk of appearing gullible, incompetent or intellectually naïve in the eyes of his colleagues.

Psychoanalysis is essentially a cure "effected by love,"

Freud writes to Jung in 1906. But to share authority with women and draw on their experience as a basis for science is to go against the grain of a patriarchal culture. In privileging women's voices over the voices of fathers, Freud placed his claims to manhood in jeopardy, a danger heightened in the Vienna of this period by his being a Jew. As a Jewish man, he was caught between the promise of political liberalism and the terrors of an aggressive political anti-Semitism, a dilemma Carl Schorske describes in *Fin de Siècle Vienna*. Schorske specifically situates *The Interpretation of Dreams* in

> Freud's life-long struggle with Austrian socio-political reality, as scientist and Jew, as citizen and son. In *The Interpretation of Dreams*, Freud gives this struggle, both outer and inner, its fullest, most personal state-ment—and at the same time overcame it by devising an epoch-making interpretation of human experience in which politics could be reduced to an epiphenomenal manifestation of psychic forces. (p. 183)

Freud regarded his dream book as his most important and path-breaking scientific work. He had discovered the meaning of dreams, their function in the human psyche; he had found that dreams follow a distinctive psychological logic, associative rather than deductive, and that this logic could be deciphered through the dreamer's associations. Schorske, however, shows that the work is both personal and political, drawing its data base from Freud's highly autobiographical dreams at a time when he was struggling with the death of his father and the frustration of his own professional ambitions.

Read as a developmental narrative, the Oedipus

tragedy offers an explanation for a psychology that naturalizes the dissociation, the splitting of consciousness, that even in Freud's time had come to be associated with trauma. Suspended in the unconscious, Oedipus becomes a template of dissociation disguised as a manifestation of our deepest wishes and fears. In his hysterical patients, Freud had observed a kind of healthy resistance to the codes of patriarchal womanhood, noting as "typical of the features one meets with so frequently in hysterical people" their giftedness, their moral sensibility, and "an independence of nature that went beyond the feminine ideal and found expression in a considerable amount of obstinacy, pugnacity and reserve" (*Studies on Hysteria*, p. 161). When they could not speak directly about what they knew through experience, they turned to the indirect discourse of symptoms. The most common symptom of hysteria, the loss of voice, carried the political message: I have been silenced.

But the silencing of women had become essential for Freud's theory. Blinding himself like Oedipus and, like Oedipus, summoning his daughter to accompany him in his blindness, Freud shows us the power of fantasy to override reality when he writes that women must accept "the fact of their castration." His early sense of reaching the headwaters of neurosis came from linking women's neurotic suffering with the pathology of fathers, the otherwise respectable men implicated in incestuous relationships with their daughters. To ask what explained this unnatural turn in the sexual lives and loves of fathers, and also to inquire into the silence or complicity of mothers, would lead to an explanation at once psychological and political. In the daughters' physical symptoms, we see the refusal of a resisting voice to go gently into silence. Yet with the Oedipus Complex, Freud has naturalized patriarchy, and liberal political resistance becomes one among many signs of father–son or father–daughter conflict.

The quotation from the *Aeneid* that Freud chose as the epigraph for *The Interpretation of Dreams* expresses Juno's rage at the upper world, at Jupiter, for driving Aeneas away from Dido and Carthage. He was leaving love and shared rule with a woman to resume his mission of founding Rome and thus allay the doubts cast on his manhood. The evolution of Freud's theory from *Studies on Hysteria* to *The Interpretation of Dreams* suggests a similar trajectory. Freud's ambition and his sense of manhood had been assaulted by anti-Semitism. In stereotypes prevalent at the time, Jewish men were cast as at once effeminate and highly sexed. Against this background, we can understand Freud's shift from his early alliance with women and the central role he accorded sexuality to the established "normal" misogyny of his later views and his increasing focus on aggression, which he naturalized as a "death instinct." If his goal was to secure psychoanalysis and gain stature within a conventionally patriarchal, Christian society, this can be seen as a necessary move. Yet with this move, psychoanalysis lost its radical edge.

The tension between psychoanalysis and the surrounding culture now lodged within psychoanalysis itself; its method and its theory were fundamentally at odds. In freeing association, Freud had discovered a way to release the psyche from the grip of patriarchy. With

96

his Oedipus theory, he re-inscribed patriarchy into the psyche. The tension between a liberating method and a suppressive theory settled into the relationship between analyst and patient, and the difficulty of resolving this tension may explain why analyses so often became interminable.

The Oedipus legend is a trauma story that plays out across generations. As myth, it is a symbolic representation of wishes and fantasies that beset the psyche in patriarchy: to retaliate against a father who put his own interests over that of his child, to sexually possess a mother who abandoned her child in aligning herself with a father's agenda. As a thumbprint of a patriarchal civilization, the Oedipus myth does indeed reveal its tragedy.

The novelist Gish Jen observes that when a fascist regime comes to power the first thing they do is get rid of the artists. Then they close the libraries. Our inner lives and our history must become a mystery. In the thirty-first of his *New Introductory Lectures on Psycho-Analysis*, written in 1933, Freud turns to "The Dissection of the Psychical Personality." His subject is the ego, the I, but he warns the ladies and gentlemen in his imagined audience that he is going deal with it in an unaccustomed manner. Starting with a notion he assumes to be familiar, he observes that "pathology, by making things larger and coarser, can draw our attention to normal conditions which would otherwise have escaped us. Where it points to a breach or a rent, there may normally be an articulation present" (pp. 58–9). With a striking image, he illustrates the point:

If we throw a crystal to the floor, it breaks; but not into haphazard pieces. It comes apart along its lines of cleavage into fragments whose boundaries, though they were invisible, were predetermined by the crystal's structure. Mental patients are split and broken structures of this same kind. (p. 59)

In neurotic patients, Freud had observed the fragmentation of the psyche: the splits in consciousness, the divisions between mind and body, emotion and thought. In the hermetic chamber of the analytic setting, he had encouraged his patients to bring a hidden self into relationship—with the analyst and with themselves. His method of free association restored psychic wholeness as previously dissociated parts of the self—repressed memories, insights, and desires—were brought back into consciousness and met with human understanding or, as Freud says, with love. Love and the truth set people free.

In his lecture, Freud goes on to say that neurotic sufferers had "turned away from external reality, but for that very reason they know more about internal, psychical reality and can reveal a number of things to us that would otherwise be inaccessible to us" (p. 59). The shattered psyches of neurotic patients lay bare a fragmentation that was predetermined—and here was the catch. What had caused this fragmentation?

Freud knew, but his knowledge had put him in what became for him an untenable position. He was caught between a rock and a hard place. His most creative voice as a psychologist had emerged in his early relationships with women; his credibility and his manhood hinged on breaking these relationships. Freeing association, he then bound it to his Oedipus theory. Even the most creative men of the highest integrity and intelligence often cannot bear the pressures on their honor as men and need to establish their manhood in the eyes of other men. Thus Freud dissociated himself from the insights of his early work, in essence separating his love from his knowledge.

In a man with as much integrity as Freud, what is so sad and so shocking is his incorporation of a patriarchal voice into the very structure of the psyche in the form of a superego or over-I: an over-voice that speaks to the self, the I, with the force of moral authority. Thus Freud did not so much turn away from politics as write an essentially patriarchal politics into psychology to much more devastating effect.

Once patriarchy is read as nature, we do not question why sexual love is so problematic and aggression, including war, so irresistible. We cannot solve the riddle of femininity. There is no space within such a psychology for even raising the question of whether the traumatic disruption of relationship (such that people cannot desire what they love or love what they desire) is what makes male violence and the "universal tendency [by which Freud means men's tendency] to debasement in the sphere of love" ("On the Universal Tendency," p. 179) so endemic and pervasive. Both war and tragic love come to seem, as it were, in the nature of things. Reading the history of culture in a way that aligns a patriarchal psychology with civilization, we see its discomfort or neurosis as the price we have to pay.

Yet the trauma story lingers.

A split now enters psychoanalysis. There are two trauma stories, but only one is told as such. Considering

99

the experience of men in war, Freud writes about "war trauma" and collects the essays of his followers (including Ferenczi) who had had experience as military psychiatrists. In *Symptoms, Inhibitions, and Anxiety* (1926), he sees objective anxiety as primary. Freud never denied the existence of childhood sexual abuse or its adverse effects, as some have claimed. Working with populations, girls and boys, displaced during World War I, the Hungarian psychiatrists in Budapest (not just Ferenczi but the whole group based at St. Elizabeth's Hospital) write about trauma (among psychotics as well as neurotics), and August Aichhorn does the same in Vienna (his *Wayward Youth*, published in 1925, was much admired by Freud). Although Melanie Klein follows Freud in positing a death instinct to explain the pervasiveness of aggression, the young social democrats (Wilhelm Reich, Otto Fenichel, Annie Reich, and Edith Jacobson among others) argue that "the environment"—meaning adverse social conditions and familial frustrations—moves people to fight and go to war, not an inborn drive. Following World War II, as the contemporary psychoanalysts Elisabeth Young-Bruehl and Christine Dunbar remind us,

> Anna Freud recorded the effects of trauma in her Hampstead War Nurseries report, as Bowlby wrote about the effects of wartime separations on children, as Winnicott shifted away from his initial Kleinian theoretical allegiance to stress environmental effects (and to speak of "the environmental mother").

There are real traumas in life, and people suffer from them.

100

Yet women's stories of childhood sexual abuse or adolescent violation continued to be questioned. When it came to women, the emphasis on fantasy rather than reality persisted after Freud's death and for decades following World War II. Women were a thorn in the flesh for the Oedipus theory. And psychoanalysts, skeptical by profession, aligned for the most part with the position Freud had taken in 1897, the year after his father's death. Writing to Wilhelm Fliess, his confidante, he says that he no longer believes his theory linking neurosis with trauma because there are "no indications of reality in the unconscious, so that one cannot distinguish between truth and fiction that has been cathected with affect" (*Complete Letters*, p. 264). The implication is that with something as charged as sexual trauma, there is no way of knowing what actually happened. The voices of daughters are pitted against the reputations of fathers, and Freud takes what is in effect a hands-off stance.

Here we witness the theoretical shift from speaking about dissociation to speaking about the unconscious, or more accurately, a change in the understanding of the unconscious itself. Within psychoanalysis, there are two ways to think about the unconscious. One is to see it as the place where all the repressed or dissociated memories, insights, and wishes go. They are then out of awareness—unconscious—but they can be brought back into awareness through association. The other view regards the unconscious as the locus of inborn drives, a region apart, as hell is separated from purgatory and heaven in medieval paintings. Steam may rise, but it is not possible to go there in this life. In this view, an interpreter is needed—a psychoanalyst-priest.

In Freud's revised conception, the unconscious becomes accessible only through interpretation. We watch the formation of a priesthood: the interpreters who stand between the patient and his/her unconscious. And we see a democratic method, grounded in equal voice, yield to hierarchy, as the interpreters, the psychoanalysts, now assume the position of authority.

The voices of resistance within psychoanalysis focused on traumas associated with war, social dislocation, and family dysfunction (especially bad mothering). There were moves toward a paradigm shift as the emphasis on sexual and aggressive drives or life and death instincts gave way to the recognition that we have an inborn desire for relationships and human attachment is primary (rather than a derivative of sexual drives).

Still, the trauma embedded in the Oedipus legend could not be named. Freud's omission of the Laius prelude was noticed by Marianne Krull in *Freud and His Father*, and before that by George Devereux, the psychoanalytically trained anthropologist, but the Laius pre-history was not restored. In psychoanalytic thinking, the Oedipus Complex remains for the most part something inherent in human development rather than something that develops in a patriarchal culture: a product of repression and, more particularly, the repression of boys' desires for emotional closeness and their identification with their mothers. Psychoanalysts had written trauma into the psyche, and the psyche then bore the stamp of tragedy. Psyche and Eros, the mythic couple who represent the joining of the soul with love, were displaced by Oedipus and Thanatos, and Pleasure (the daughter of Psyche and Eros) gave way to loss and the compulsion to repeat.

But we also see a displacement in the very telling of the incest story. The shift in emphasis from reality to fantasy in psychoanalytic theory follows a switch in the narrator of the incest story. Rather than listening to the young woman recount her experience of an incestuous relationship with her father, we hear the young boy fantasizing about an incestuous relationship with his mother. By privileging the boy, his fantasy overrides the woman's reality—or, more insidiously, by assimilating the voices of women to the Oedipus theory and focusing on the unconscious, the line between reality and fantasy blurs. We are in the underworld with Aeneas, where "sees" becomes "thinks to have seen," in a world of shades and phantoms.

From this point on, psychoanalytic theory will be at risk from women's voices that are not captive to a father's voice or bound to a patriarchal story.

ACT III

The time is the 1970s. Enter women who again take center stage, not as patients but as psychologists who, in the spirit of the times, are questioning authority.

Beginning in the 1970s, the lens of gender brought into sharp focus a psychology so wedded to patriarchy that the omission of women from its research studies had for the most part not been seen, or if seen, had not been considered consequential. It was an omission "so obvious that no one noticed," to borrow a phrase from Arundhati Roy's novel, *The God of Small Things*. That it turned out to be no small thing was the discovery

of research that started with women and extended to
girls, to boys, and to a reconsideration of what had
been taken as true about men. Women, enjoined by
patriarchy to be selfless, to be responsive to others but
to silence themselves, were holding up half of the sky.
The longstanding and vaunted divisions between mind
and body, reason and emotion, self and relationship,
when viewed through the lens of gender, turned out
to be deeply gendered, reflecting the binaries and hierarchies of a patriarchal culture. These gendered splits
create a chasm in human nature, deforming both men's
and women's natures. One consequence was an argument over which half was better—the masculine or the
feminine part. But the argument itself was based on false
premises. The problem lay in the paradigm itself.

In the classical manner of scientific advances, the
discrepant data—the evidence that did not fit the reigning patriarchal construction—proved most informative.
Thus women's voices were privileged in informing psychologists about aspects of the human condition that
(by being tagged feminine and associated with women)
had been at once ignored and devalued. A paradigm
shift followed from this research, joining together what
had been split asunder. Whereas in the old paradigm,
women were seen as emotional not rational, as having
relationships but no self, and men, conversely, were
considered rational insofar as they were unemotional
and autonomous in their sense of self, the new paradigm
undid the splits. The origin of these insights lay in the
different voices of women—different insofar as they
were resisting these splits by asserting the relational
nature of all human experience.

Free Association and the Grand Inquisitor

As the paradigm shift released voices in both women and men that previously could not be heard or understood, the early insights of Freud were retrieved along with those of Ferenczi, Suttie, Winnicott and others in a reframing of psychology that came increasingly to focus on dissociation and trauma. Studies of women, of babies and mothers, and new research on boys and men led to a remapping of development. And in this light, the requisites of love and the consequences of traumatic loss became clear.

But it was the research with girls that elucidated more radically an intersection where psychological development collides with the demands of patriarchy, its gender norms and roles and values. The research highlighted what had previously been taken as a stage in the normal course of development and showed it to be a process of initiation, the induction of the psyche into patriarchy. The most telling finding stemmed from the observation that girls entering adolescence show signs of a resistance not to growing up but to losing their minds, as thirteen-year-old Judy put it. The crisis was one of relationship and the resistance was to the split between voice and relationship. Paradoxically, girls were discovering that their honest voices were jeopardizing their relationships, not only their personal relationships but also their connection to the culture they were entering as young women. The initiation into patriarchy required a breaking of relationship, a sacrifice of love for the sake of honor or advancement.

It was this sacrifice that girls resisted in entering womanhood, and the trajectory of their resistance drew attention to the various meanings of the word: resistance in the sense of resistance to disease; resistance as political resistance—speaking truth to power; and resistance in its psychoanalytic connotation as a reluctance to bring into consciousness things kept out of awareness. In the scene mentioned earlier from *A Streetcar Named Desire*, where Stella tells Eunice that she could not believe her sister and go on living with her husband, she captures the dilemma of living in patriarchy. It is necessary not to believe or to know what is happening in order to join a culture that requires repression, where, as in Tennessee Williams' play, the streetcar named Desire leads to the insane asylum.

It is hard now for me to recapture that first elation that my graduate students and I experienced in discovering that we have within ourselves, within our very nature, the capacities for voice and relationship that are the foundation for both love and democratic politics. Adolescent girls would come to label an honest voice "stupid"—insufferable or unpleasant, wrong or crazy— just as boys, at an earlier time in their development (the time Freud marked as the Oedipal period) would come to hear an emotionally open voice as "babyish"; associating their relational desires and vulnerabilities with mothers, they would forsake them as unmanly. And yet the striking finding both with adolescent girls and with boys, in the preschool years and also at adolescence, lay in the evidence of a resistance that was associated with psychological resilience or health. This resistance makes trouble in the sense of challenging the necessity or the value of losses that have come to be taken as in the very nature of things or seen as sacrifices to be made in the interest of growing up and finding one's place in society.

In the 1990s, these insights from studies of psychological development were extended by discoveries in neurobiology, heralded by the publication of Antonio Damasio's widely acclaimed *Descartes' Error: Emotion, Reason, and the Human Brain*. As developmental research had revealed the splits between self and relationships to signal a traumatic disruption of human connection, so neurological studies revealed the split between reason and emotion to signal trauma or brain injury. We had, we learned, been wedded to a false story about ourselves, through a process illuminated by Damasio in *The Feeling of What Happens: Body and Emotion in the Making of Consciousness*.

Exploring the neurological foundations of consciousness, Damasio distinguished core consciousness or a "core sense of self," grounded in the body and in emotion, from what he called the "autobiographical self," the self that is wedded to a story about itself. We are wired neurologically to register our experience from moment to moment in our bodies and our emotions, like a film running continually inside us, and our awareness of watching the film extends the sense of self through time and history, leading to memory and identity. Thus in our bodies and our emotions, we record the music or the feeling of what happens, which then plays in our minds, our thoughts.

By bringing the lens of gender to the distinction between a core self, grounded in the body and in emotion, and an autobiographical self wedded to a story about itself, we can see more precisely how an initiation that splits mind from body and reason from emotion can wed us to a false story about ourselves—a story

107

false in its representation of both women and men. But we also understand how and why free association can unbind us from that false story by releasing the voice of the core self. The voice of experience then can counter a voice of false authority. Hence our ability to spot a false story.

In an informal seminar for Ph.D. students at the University of Cambridge, one of the students presents her research. She is studying mothers of infants and she describes how oppressed they feel by the idealization of motherhood in the mandatory course given by the National Health Service. I ask the five women in this all-women seminar (only one of whom was at that time a mother) what they know about life with a young baby in the house. Growing up, they experienced the birth of siblings. They remember short tempers, sleep-deprived parents, crying babies, and mess. Why then, I ask, do women lend credence to what they know is a false story about motherhood? Why don't they listen to what they know on the basis of experience to be true? The focus of the research shifted.

Here again, the research with girls is instructive, underscoring the insight in Apuleius's telling of the story of Eros and Psyche—a story about love and the soul. Like Psyche, girls and women can play a critical role in resisting the Love Laws of patriarchy if they refuse the objectification of women, the idealization and denigration, and break prohibitions on seeing and saying what they know through experience to be true about men and about love.

A gender lens then hones the perception that because the initiation of girls into the codes and scripts of patriarchal manhood and womanhood tends to occur at adolescence rather than around the ages of four or five, because it is in adolescence (rather than early childhood) that girls are pressed to take on a father's voice as the voice of moral authority and to live by the law of the father, girls have more resources to draw on in resisting the trauma, the loss of voice and the dissociation. In fighting for real relationship, women are joined by men who are similarly moved to resist patriarchal constraints on love. It is in this sense that adolescence becomes a second chance for boys when erotic desire and an enhanced subjectivity move them to reveal what they may have repressed or hidden—their emotional intelligence, their tenderness—and thus to reject patriarchal constructions of manhood, as Eros does in exposing his love for Psyche.

Our ability to love and to live with a sense of psychic wholeness hinges on our ability to resist wedding ourselves to the gender binaries of patriarchy. That this capacity for resistance is grounded in our neurobiology heightens the importance of a developmental psychology that provides us with an accurate map with which to chart our course. Once we see where we have come from, we can recognize more clearly the alternative routes we might follow—one marked by Oedipus and leading to the birth of tragedy, and the other by the resistance of Psyche and Eros and leading to the birth of pleasure.

ACT IV

The time is now. The characters Christ and the Grand Inquisitor.

In *The Brothers Karamazov*, Ivan, the nihilist, tells his saintly brother Alyosha of a prose poem he has written. It is set in sixteenth-century Spain at the height of the Inquisition. Almost a hundred heretics had, *ad majorem gloriam Dei*, been burned by the cardinal, the Grand Inquisitor, "in a 'splendid *auto da fe*', in the presence of the king, the court, knights, cardinals, and the loveliest court ladies, before the teeming populace of all Seville" (p. 248). On the day following this conflagration, Christ appears, having returned to earth and reassuming his human form: "He appeared quietly, inconspicuously, but, strange to say, everyone recognized him."

"This could be one of the best passages in the poem," Ivan says.

> I mean, why it is exactly that they recognize him. People are drawn to him by an invincible force, they flock to him, surround him, follow him. He passes silently among them with a quiet smile of infinite compassion. The sun of love shines in his heart, rays of Light, Enlightenment, and Power stream from his eyes and, pouring over the people, shake their hearts with responding love. He stretches forth his hands to them, blesses them, and from the touch of him, even only of his garments, comes a healing power. (p. 249)

He restores sight to the blind, life to the dead. "There is commotion among the people, cries, weeping, and at this very moment the Cardinal Grand Inquisitor himself crosses the square in front of the cathedral." Witnessing what is happening,

> he stretches forth his finger and orders the guard to take him. And such is his power, so tamed, submissive, and

tremblingly obedient to his will are the people, that the
crowd immediately parts before the guard, and they,
amidst the deathly silence that has suddenly fallen, lay
their hands on him and lead him away. (pp. 249–50)

That night, the air "fragrant with laurel and lemon,"
the Grand Inquisitor visits his prisoner, entering the cell
with a light in his hand and gazing into his face. Then
slowly he sets the light on the table and asks: "Is it you?
You?" Receiving no answer, he quickly adds,

Do not answer, be silent. After all, what could you say? I
know too well what you would say . . . tomorrow I shall
condemn you and burn you at the stake as the most evil
of heretics, and the very people who today kissed your
feet, tomorrow, at a nod from me, will rush to heap the
coals up around your stake. (p. 250)

He tells the silent Jesus, "We corrected your deed and
based it on *miracle, mystery, and authority*." And then
he says, "Tell me, were we right in teaching and doing
so?" (p. 257).

My drama ends without resolution, but the question
is clear. In discovering the power of free association,
psychoanalysis gained the ability to free people from dissociation by connecting their love with their knowledge.
With the Oedipus theory, this promise was constrained.
With the shift in emphasis from reality to fantasy a
cure through love became wedded to miracle, mystery,
and authority. Patients, once seen to know everything
that was of any pathogenic significance relating to their
symptoms, became captive to the analyst, whose authority lay in a seemingly miraculous power to interpret the

111

mysteries of the unconscious. In the late twentieth century, as the winds of liberation swept through society, the authority of psychoanalysis was questioned and its patriarchal underpinnings exposed. Free association, it turned out, had been bound to the voice and law of the father.

The Grand Inquisitor's question then becomes a question for our time. Was he right in his assessment that people find love and freedom too burdensome? How do we think about our own lives and relationships? How do we see ourselves?

As the tale of "The Emperor's New Clothes" attests, children are by nature lie-resistant. The four-year-old boy who asks his mother, "Mommy, why are you sad?" and then responds to her denial of sadness by saying, "Mommy I know you, I was inside you," and the eleven-year-old girl who observed, "My house is wallpapered with lies," sound a voice that resides within all of us, however buried. The power of free association lies in its ability to release this voice from the forces that would confuse and constrain it. The tensions within psychoanalysis, its practice and its institutional arrangements, mirror the ongoing contradictions between democracy and patriarchy and reflect the dissonance between a voice grounded in the body and in emotion and a voice that is wed to a false story.

More than ever, we need psychoanalysis with its method of free association to undo the dissociations that currently threaten not only our happiness but also our survival. But we need a psychoanalysis freed from its truncated Oedipus story, a psychoanalysis that recognizes trauma as the force that turns love into incest and anger to murder, a psychoanalysis that is at once psychological and political—that joins our healthy resistance to the temptations of miracle, mystery, and authority, and encourages us to take the risk of opting for love and freedom.

4 Identifying the Resistance

I. In the museum

It is Tuesday. It is raining. And I am going to the Boston Museum of Fine Arts with eight eleven-year-old girls, members of the sixth grade at the Atrium School in Watertown, Massachusetts. We climb into the school van and begin to make our way through rain-dark streets into the city. It is June. School is over for the year. The sixth grade has graduated, and the girls from the class have returned for a week of outings, writing, and theater work designed to strengthen healthy resistance and courage. They gather in the coatroom of the museum, shedding backpacks and raincoats, retrieving notebooks: they are ready. Today, I explain, we are going to be investigative reporters: our assignment is to find out how women appear in this museum.

"Naked," Emma says without hesitation. A current of recognition passes swiftly through the group. Like Dora, Freud's patient who stood in the Dresden art gallery for two-and-a-half hours in front of the Sistine

114

Madonna, Emma will be transfixed by the images of women, by their nakedness in this cool, marble building. Later, when asked to write a conversation with one of the women in the museum, she chooses a headless, armless Greek statue, weaving into the conventions of polite conversation her two burning questions: "Are you cold?" and "Would you like some clothes?"

Emma's playfully innocent, slightly irreverent conversation with the statue in the museum bespeaks her interest in the scenes that lie behind the paintings and sculptures she is seeing—an inquiry into relationships between artists and models: what each is doing and feeling and thinking; a curiosity about the psychological dimensions of this connection between women and men. The statue's response—"I have no money"—to the question of whether she wants some clothes, reveals how readily this inquiry becomes political, and sets up the dynamic I wish to follow: the tendency in girls' lives at adolescence for a resistance that is inherently political—an insistence on knowing what one knows and a willingness to be outspoken—to turn into a psychological resistance, a reluctance to know what one knows and a fear that one's knowledge, if spoken, will endanger relationships and threaten survival.

I return for a moment to the museum to record the doubling of voice and vision that characterized the girls' perceptions and conversations. Mame's eye for the disparity between outside and inside, between calm surface and explosive laughter, is evident as she describes the painting of "Reverend John Atwood and his family." His two oldest daughters, she writes, "have no expression. They're just staring straight ahead, but one of them looks like she is going to burst out laughing." His wife, she concludes on a more somber note, "looks very worn and tired." By paying attention to the human world around them and following the changing weather of relationships and the undercurrents of thoughts and emotions, girls come to discern patterns. They notice repeating sequences and hear familiar rhythms, and thus find under the apparent disorder of everyday living an order that is the psychological equivalent of the Mandelbrot equations of chaos physics.

Yet girls' "unpaid-for-education"—Virginia Woolf's name for "that understanding of human beings and their motives which ... might be called psychology" (*Three Guineas*, p. 9)—leaves them with knowledge that often runs counter to what they are told by those in authority. So they are left, in effect, with at least two truths, two versions of a story, two voices revealing different points of view. Malka, perhaps reflecting her bi-cultural Cuban-American heritage, writes not one but two conversations between herself and the Queen of Babylon. The first is the official version. Speaking in the voice of a reporter, Malka addresses the Queen in a manner befitting her station. "Hello Madam," she says to the woman in the painting who is brushing her hair while receiving news of the revolt. "What is it like ruling so great a land?" "Glorious," the Queen replies, "it is great fun although," she adds with a yawn, "it does tax time and strength sometimes." In the second conversation, Malka speaks in her own voice to this bored, haughty Queen, asking her simply: "Whatchya doing?" The Queen, in a sudden reversal of priorities, replies:

"Brushing my hair. I was interrupted this morning by a revolt."

Whose agenda, what is important, what can be spoken and what is tacitly to be ignored—looked at but not seen, heard but not listened to? These are questions raised by studying girls. The play of girls' conversation, the questions and comments that dart in and out like minnows, followed by looks, scanning faces, listening for what happens, seeing what follows, taking the pulse, the temperature of the human climate: Is anyone upset? What is permitted? Admitted in both senses of the word (to let in, to acknowledge or confess). Conflict erupts among girls like lightning—something has happened, someone has stepped over a line. Rejection—the thin, dark line of rejection: not you; we—whoever "we" are—do not want to be with you.

Girls' questions about who wants to be with whom are to them among the most important questions, and they take sharp notice throughout the day of the answers given to these questions as revealed through nuance and gesture, voice and glances, seating arrangements, choices of partners, the responses of women and men, the attitude of authorities in the world. Emma's voice in saying that the nudes are naked, Mame's voice in speaking about the irreverence of the daughter and the tiredness of the mother in Reverend John Atwood's family, Malka's voice in revealing by reversing the relationship between hair-brushing and quelling revolts, are the same three voices that Anne Frank suppresses in editing her diary.

On March 28, 1944, in a broadcast by Radio Free Orange from London into the Netherlands, Anne learns of plans by the Dutch government in exile to set up a War Museum after the war. Gerrit Bolkestein, the minister of education, art, and science, speaks of their interest in diaries, letters, and collections of sermons that would show how the Dutch people carried on their lives under the extreme conditions of the war. Anne dreamed of becoming a famous writer, and she seizes her chance. In the short time between May and August of 1944, when the Gestapo raided the Secret Annex, she rewrites 324 pages of her diary, reaching March of '44 in her edited version. When Miep Geis, the courageous and openhearted friend who had sustained the Franks in hiding, gathered up the scattered notebooks and loose pages from the disarray left by the Nazis, she found most of both the actual diary and Anne's edited version. After the war, when Otto Frank prepared his daughter's diary for publication, he followed her editing with a few notable exceptions, presenting his daughter to the world as she wished to be seen.

Anne was aware of living in hiding, but not only from the Nazis. Writing to Kitty, the fictitious friend to whom she addresses her diary, the friend in whom she can "confide . . . completely" (p. 177), she confesses, "I hid myself within myself . . . and quietly wrote down all my joys, sorrows and contempt in my diary" (p. 438). When compared with her actual diary, her edited version, prepared for the Museum, makes clear what she wished to keep hidden: that she had looked at and seen her own naked body, that she and her mother and sister were "thick as thieves," and that she knew from her reading what activities people record and imbue with value and was disturbed by the disparate attention given to men's and women's courage and suffering. On June 15, 1944, at the age of fifteen, she writes:

> A question that has been raised more than once and that gives me no inner peace is why did so many nations in the past, and often still now, treat women as inferior to men? Everyone can agree how unjust this is, but that is not enough for me I would also like to know the cause of the great injustice . . . It is stupid enough of women to have borne it all in silence for such a long time, since the more centuries this arrangement lasts, the more deeply rooted it becomes . . . Many people, particularly women, but also men, now realize for how long this state of affairs has been wrong, and modern women demand the right of complete independence! But that's not all, respect for women, that's going to have to come as well! . . . Soldiers and war heroes are honored and celebrated, explorers acquire immortal fame, martyrs are revered, but how many will look upon woman as they would upon a soldier? . . . Women are much braver, much more courageous soldiers, struggling and enduring pain for the continuance of humankind, than all the freedom-fighting heroes with their big mouths! (p. 678)

That girls' knowledge—of the body, of relationships, and of the world and its values—and girls' irreverence provide the grounds for resistance has been known since the time of *Lysistrata*.

II. If only women . . .

In 411 B.C.E., in the midst of the disastrous war between Athens and Sparta, Aristophanes lays out a plan for ending the war in a bawdy comedy, *Lysistrata*. If only women, Lysistrata thinks, who are able to see the absurdity of men's fighting, who are wise moreover in the ways of human bodies and psyches, and who can have an effect on men, would take the salvation of Greece into their hands, they could, she imagines, stop the violence. At the opening of the play, Lysistrata calls the women of Athens and Sparta together, preparing to explain her plan. In this classical rendition of peace-making women, the voices and expression of these women resonate with the voices and gestures of eleven-year-old girls in the late twentieth century.

"I am angry . . . I am very angry and upset," Sarah says, protesting with her whole face and body. Somberness gathers across her eyebrows, joining them as she says directly: "I was treated by Ted [their sixth grade teacher] like trash." Tension is in the air. Sarah and Emma walk back and forth across the room, heads down, arms around each other's shoulders. The atmosphere darkens, hurt feelings move in, sudden shadows, tears, then talking, contact, an opening, light and shadow, the play of relationships, the somberness that gathered across Sarah's face moves off. Sarah and Emma line up chairs, dragging them into rows, two chairs apiece, bottoms on one, feet on another. They open their journals and begin writing.

"What's bothering you Lysistrata?" Calonice asks at the beginning of Act One in Alan Sommerstein's 1973 Penguin Classics translation. "Don't screw up your face like that. It really doesn't suit you, knitting your eyebrows up like a bow." "Sorry, Calonice, but I'm furious. I'm disappointed in womankind." Lysistrata is upset because the women of Athens and Sparta have not shown up for her meeting—and she knows they would do so for Bacchus. Taking on the task of speaking to someone who is too angry to listen, Calonice reminds Lysistrata, "It is not so easy for a wife to get out of the house."

When the women do finally come, Lysistrata explains that if the women will vow to give up sex until men vow to give up fighting, they should succeed in bringing about peace—in essence substituting the mutual pleasures of sex for men's single-minded pursuit of honor. The strategy is as follows: the women will do everything in their power to arouse their husbands and lovers, and then run out of their houses and lock themselves up in the Acropolis. This plan succeeds brilliantly in the theater. The Peloponnesian War, however, continues.

More than two millennia later in a novel set in Puritan New England, Hawthorne puts forward a similar vision: a woman must bring the "new truth . . . in order to establish the whole relation between man and woman on a surer ground of mutual happiness" (*The Scarlet Letter*, p. 241). And then, in a stunning exegesis, with the brilliant economy of the letter A, he demonstrates why this vision is doomed to failure. The very passion that renders a woman *able* to see through the "iron framework" of Puritanism also disables her by causing her to be seen in the eyes of the Puritans as an impure woman, a woman who has been *adulterated*.

This double vision that at once frees and imprisons women is explicated in "Another View of Hester," following the scene where seven-year-old Pearl offers another view of the Reverend Arthur Dimmesdale

("Thou wast not bold!—thou wast not true! . . . Thou wouldst not promise to take my hand, and mother's hand, to-morrow noontide!") (p. 142). The scarlet letter that reveals Hester's passion also gives her "so much power to do, and power to sympathize,—that many people refused to interpret the scarlet A by its original signification. They said that it meant Able; so strong was Hester Prynne, with a woman's strength" (p. 146).

Living at once inside and outside the framework, Hester is able to see the frame. Her "lawless passion" set her mind free, leading to speculations which, the narrator surmises, the Puritan forefathers "would have held to be a deadlier crime than that stigmatized by the scarlet letter" (p. 149) because they threaten the foundations of the Puritan order. What was taken as God given was, Hester realizes, a human construction; built up in one way, it could "be torn down, and built up anew" (p. 150). Men of the sword had overthrown nobles and kings (the novel is set in the year the English king was beheaded). Yet in order for women "to assume what seems a fair and suitable position" in society, "the very nature of the opposite sex, or its long hereditary habit, which has become like nature, is to be essentially modified." And that of woman too (woman "cannot take advantage of these preliminary reforms, until she herself shall have undergone a still mightier change" [p. 150]). The realization of a political vision, the promise of a fair and just society, hinges on a psychological transformation—a task Hester discerns to be more daunting than overthrowing nobles and kings because it requires a change in what has come to seem "like nature."

Like the hysterical women of the late nineteenth

century, Hester Prynne has the character of a resister: "a mind of native courage and activity" (p. 183), a woman whom fate and fortune had set free:

> The scarlet letter was her passport into regions where other women dared not tread. Shame, Despair, Solitude! These had been her teachers,—stern and wild ones,— and they had made her strong, but taught her much amiss. (pp. 183–4)

In the end, then, she must be corrected, and unlike Dora—Freud's patient who flees from what had become the iron framework of his treatment, leaving her analysis in mid-stream—Hester, in the dark conclusion of Hawthorne's brooding novel, reassumes the Puritan mantle. She assures the women who come to her for counsel and comfort that there will be a new order of living between women and men, grounded not in sorrow but in mutual happiness. She knows that "the angel and apostle of the coming revelation must be a woman" and had once imagined this prophetess might be herself. But the angel must be "lofty [and] pure" as well as beautiful, wise "not through dusky grief, but the ethereal medium of joy . . . and sacred love" (p. 241). Hawthorne thus captures the catch-22 of feminism: the very woman who is able to envision a new order of living is, by the same token, unable, since the passion that enables her also adulterates her in the eyes of the Puritans. Released from goodness, she is imprisoned in badness, within the framework of a puritanical order. But her mind is free to question the order.

The imprisonment of women is the subject of Claudia Koonz's scathing jeremiad—her 1987 study of women in Nazi Germany, *Mothers in the Fatherland*. Koonz asks a question that rivets many people: how could women, how could mothers especially, have stayed with and supported such fathers? Interviewing Gertrud Scholtz-Klink, the "Lady Fuhrer über Alles," chief of the Women's Bureau—the oxymoronic Nazi social service agency—and author of *Women in the Third Reich*, Koonz is spellbound by her protestations of goodness, by a moral piety and smugness that seemingly admit no pity. "Crimefeel" is the term she coins for this unrepentant woman's insistence on describing herself as both a good mother and a good Nazi—the emotional analogue to the murderous "crimethink" that Orwell describes in *Nineteen Eighty-Four*. The fact is that women did not resist Hitler in any more significant numbers than did members of the caring professions: doctors, clergy, and educators. This is surprising only in that the main form that resistance could take under the relentless eye of Nazi terror was, it would seem, characteristically feminine. The resistance relied on what might be considered women's ways of doing things—hiding documents under babies, wheedling information through seduction, manipulating rather than confronting. Yet women as a group did not resist but actively supported and voted into power the openly sexist and avowedly misogynistic Nazi party, with an idealization of mothers that provided only the thinnest veneer over rage and contempt. Soldiers and mothers—the imagery of Hitler's Germany; what were they doing in one another's company?

This knotted dilemma lies at the center of women's development. How can girls both enter and stay outside of, be educated in and then try to change, what for millennia has been a man's world? And yet since our public and private worlds are inseparably connected, since we live in one world and cannot dissociate ourselves from one another, and since the psychology of fathers which has ruled the private house is writ large in legal codes and moral commandments and supported by what is considered a legitimate use of force, how can daughters be anywhere other than at once inside and outside these structures? The key is to hold onto both their insiders' knowledge and their outsiders' perspective.

In doubling their voices and their vision, girls do just this. They play with shifting perspectives and resist pressures to resolve contradictions by simply adopting a father's standpoint (as Mame resists the standpoint of the Reverend John Atwood). Yet it is tempting for girls to correct themselves in moving from primary to secondary education, where there are many incentives to align their voices and perceptions with traditional ways of speaking and seeing, and thus to enter without disrupting what has been called the human conversation. Once this correction is made, the framework becomes invisible, and then, in the words of one twelve-year-old girl, "you don't have to think."

In *A World Apart*, her extraordinary film about South Africa, which has the slow-motion quality of recovering memory, Shawn Slovo returns to the year 1963, the year when she was thirteen, the year her mother was taken away to prison, to consider, in the context of this difficult relationship between mother and daughter, "how to merge the politics with the personal without detracting from the importance of either." Slovo is the daughter of Ruth First, the journalist who was one of the few whites centrally involved with the African National Congress (the ANC), a woman whose militant opposition to apartheid led her to be arrested and detained twice under the ninety-day detention law by the South African government in 1963, the year of the film's action. In 1982, First was killed by a parcel bomb while working with the resistance in Mozambique.

Set at that edge in girls' development between childhood and adolescence, the film catches an angle of perception at odds with conventional ways of speaking about mothers and daughters—an angle that challenges widespread assumptions about what constitutes good and bad mothering. This shift in perspective reflects a discovery Slovo came to in making the film. As she states in her introduction to the diary she kept while writing the screen-play, she had set out to write in conventional terms about

> the relationship between a white woman, politically committed to the fight against apartheid, and her thirteen-year-old daughter, who must contend against politics for the love, care and time of her mother. Set against a backdrop of increasingly violent repression, [the film] chronicles the effects of the break-up of the family. (p. ix)

And yet Slovo made a very different film. Showing the break-up of the family, she reveals a connection between mother and daughter on a deeper level, a connection forged by the daughter's insistence on entering the emotional center of her mother's life. In the critical

126

scene, thirteen-year-old Molly literally breaks her mother's silence by opening her secret drawer and reading her
diary. She discovers what she most feared. Her mother
had "tried to leave us." She had tried to kill herself in
prison. "You don't care about us. You shouldn't have
had us," the dialogue runs.

In writing out this accusation of bad mothering (the
accusation made by Pauline Kael and other critics),
Slovo for the first time hears her mother's voice as well
as her own. The scene she had resisted writing, "the
conversation, the confrontation my mother and I had
never had," which "in life . . . was what kept us apart,"
turns out to have been "there all the time, just waiting
for the last moment" (pp. xi, 18).

The scene as written has the quality of remembering and also the ring of familiarity, resonating with
other moments when daughters fight for relationship
with mothers and mothers let them in. Then the desire
for human connection overrides the restraints on relationships between mothers and daughters imposed by
images of good and bad women and leads, in the case
of Shawn Slovo, to a reformulation of the question at a
deeper level: What does it mean to be a good mother to
an adolescent daughter coming of age in a violent and
racist society? What can women teach girls about resistance and courage and love in the face of indifference,
cruelty, and violence?

The illusion, blinding the critics but seen through by
Slovo in the film, is that mothers and daughters can live
in a world apart. The camera directs the viewer's eye
to the enclosure—the imprisonment of conventionally
good South African white mothers in their fenced-in

private houses. The message is clear: once daughters are able to see beyond their enclosure, mothers cannot stay with their daughters without joining the resistance. And daughters and mothers need to find ways to be with one another in this struggle.

The harsh, cold voice we associate with Anne Frank's writing about her mother turns out in large part to be the voice of her edited version, not her actual diary. In the diary itself she chronicles a relationship in transition and under stress, recording her pleasure with her mother and sister ("Mummy, Margot and I are thick as thieves again. It's really much better.") as well as her frustrations with them. After exploring her own body she asks her mother "What is that stub of a thing for?" but her mother claims not to know. Seeking to connect with her mother on a more adult level, Anne encounters a barrier. And it is this that leads her to turn on her mother, separating herself from a woman who, as Anne discerns, has become separated from herself.

III. Resistance

Five psychological truths:

1. What is unvoiced or unspoken, because it is out of relationship, tends to get out of perspective and to dominate psychic life. ("Give sorrow words. The grief that does not speak / Whispers the o'erfraught heart, and bids it break." [*Macbeth*]).
2. The hallmarks of loss are idealization and rage, and

128

under the rage, immense sadness. ("To want and want and want and not to have" [*To The Lighthouse*]).

3. What is dissociated or repressed—known and then not known—tends to return, and return, and return.

4. The logic of the psyche is an associative logic—the logic of dreams, poetry, and memory—as well as a formal logic of classification and control.

5. We learn the answers to our questions. Our questions shape what we know.

Anna is twelve. Tall and thin, her dark hair cut short, her green eyes look steadily out of a quiet, wary face. She raises the question: how can you tell if what people are saying is true, "if what they are saying about you, if they really mean it, or if they are just doing it to be mean, and it's hard to tell, I mean with a lot of people you can't tell how they are." She is trying to understand the difference between the surface banter of teasing, making fun, putting people down that went on among her friends (although she does not know if they were really her friends) at the public school she went to, and being mean, "really mean" or cruel. At her new school—a girls' school—Anna notices that everyone is "nice," and she feels good about herself when she is "nice to people or . . . not being mean" and she feels bad about herself when she is mean or hurts people but "sometimes you just can't help it." Anna thinks people can tell how she feels, even when "inside I'm really sad about something but outside I'm trying to be happy," because "if you're feeling sad, you just can't make yourself happy."

Malka writes about the disparity between inside and

outside after the outing club's trip to Plum Island—a beach and bird sanctuary off Boston's north shore:

> A sand castle, life on a small scale. Kingdoms rise and fall, water ebbs in and out. Channels, pools, castles, forests. The outside view. But on the inside—are babies being born? Are children playing? Are crafts being learned? Are people being married? Are battles being fought? Are people dying? Love, fun, smiling, and crying. Life. A sand castle.

At the brink of adolescence, girls draw attention to the disparity between the insider's view of life they are privy to in childhood and an outside view they become privy to at adolescence, intimating that their insider's knowledge is in danger of being washed out or giving way. The connection between inside and outside becomes explicitly a focus of attention when girls enter adolescence and find themselves subjected to a kind of voice and ear training, designed to make it clear what kind of voices people like to listen to in girls and what girls can say without being called "stupid" or "rude." On a daily basis, girls receive lessons in what they can let out and what they must keep in, if they do not want to be spoken about by others as mad or bad or simply told they are wrong. Struggling with this problem of containment, Anna says that she would like to be "just a better person or have better ways of thinking." She explains:

> Sometimes I will get really mad, and I can outburst or something, and I can't be like that ... I have to learn how to work with people because sometimes I just get really mad at people who can't understand what I am saying, and I get so exasperated. It is like, "Why can't

you just. . . ? What's wrong with you? Why can't you see this my way?" And I have to really go for what I want though. I can't let this stuff take over me. And you have to kind of have to fight to get what you want.

In essence, Anna states the problem of resistance as a problem of relationship. She feels pressure to hold herself in, "not to be like that . . . [not to] get really mad," or even worse, "outburst." At the same time, she realizes she must not let go of what she wants; "I can't let this stuff take over me."

At twelve, Anna struggles with this conflict. With her mother, she experiences the central dilemma of relationship: how to speak honestly and also stay in connection with others. When they go shopping for clothes, Anna explains,

> She will pull something out and she'll say, "Well, what do you think of it?" And then if I say I don't like it, then she'll get really mad, and she'll put it back . . . And then, she'll forget about what happens when I really give her my opinion, and then she'll say, "Tell me what you really think about it."

Eleven-year-old Tessie articulates the importance of voicing conflicts in relationships, explaining why it is necessary to "tell someone about it" so that you are "telling it from both sides" and can "hear the [other] person's point of view."

> When you are having an argument . . . and you just keep it inside and don't tell anyone, you never hear the person's point of view. And if you are telling someone about it, you are telling it from both sides and so you hear what my mother said, or what my brother said. And the other

person can say, well, you might be mad, but your mom was right, and you say, yeah, I know. So when you say it out loud, you have to listen.

Tessie also observes that fighting—by which she means verbal conflict or voicing disagreement—is good for relationships: "fighting is what makes relationships go on [in] the face of trouble, and the more fights you get in and the more it goes on . . . the stronger it gets because the more you can talk with that person." The subtlety of Tessie's understanding of how people come to know one another and what kind of knowledge is necessary if friends are not to hurt one another's feelings is evident as she explains that it is through fighting, rather than "just saying 'I'm sorry' to them," that you learn "how that person feels," and then you know how "not to hurt their feelings." Yet fights also carry with them the danger of not speaking and "then you seem to grow apart."

I emphasize this detailed, specific psychological knowledge based on careful listening and sustained observation and characterized by finely wrought distinctions—a naturalist's rendering of the human world—because girls' knowledge when brought out into the open is often dismissed as trivial or seen as transgressive, with the result that girls are repeatedly told not to speak, not to say anything, or at least not to talk in public about what they know.

Asked at twelve whether she has changed as a learner, Anna says that she has come to think about things she never thought about before, meaning things she had formerly taken for granted because "you just kind of

132

trusted the teacher," like 2 + 2 = 4, or the letters of the alphabet. "You don't just sit there and say, 'A—what a dumb letter'. You don't think about it."

Now, thinking about thinking and about different ways people "look at something," Anna says you might think someone is "crazy," but "that is their opinion . . . as long as it's not going to hurt anybody." She sees the need to respect others' opinions. Yet as a scholarship student in a private girls' school, she is aware of seeing things differently. She wonders how she fits into this world where "it's just friendly and everything is nice. It is really nice, I think," and where to her delight she is encouraged to speak—for Anna, an irresistible invitation. "Most of the time," she concludes at twelve, "I'm in a pretty good mood, and sometimes I'm not. Sometimes I am mad at the world."

A year later, when Anna is interviewed at thirteen, as an eighth grader, her interview is peppered with "I don't know" (spoken now over twice as many times as in the previous year, increasing from twenty-one times at age twelve to sixty-seven at thirteen, with no corresponding increase in the length of the interview transcript). Anna is fighting her reluctance to know what she knows and her inclination to suppress her voice and go along with the group. Asked about whether she has work that she loves, this child who loves learning and loves school says, "reading and singing . . . and I can just sort of get lost in them and not have to think about things." Talking about herself as a knower, she observes that "you can interpret things differently" and describes the way thoughts and feelings cascade differently from different beginnings, so that depending on where you start from—for example, in interpreting a poem—you arrive at different endpoints.

But conformity has a hold on Anna. She feels herself a member of her new school, not only a top student but also a part of her class. She watches others to see which way to go and does not, she says, "massively disagree on anything." With friends, if she disagreed, she would be "kind of mad at myself, have kind of a messed up feeling." With adults, "they would overpower me most of the time." Anna is learning to bring herself into line with the world around her. She aligns with others so as not to mess up relationships with friends or experience the helplessness of being overpowered by adults. Paradoxically, for the sake of relationships and also to protect herself, she is disconnecting herself from others.

At fourteen, in ninth grade, Anna bursts out. She draws the interviewer's attention to the change she hears in her voice: "I used to be really quiet and shy and everything, and now I am really loud." Again the phrase "I don't know" has doubled (from 67 to 135), but it alternates now with the phrase "you know" and punctuates a tale of resistance that is clearly political: an insistence on knowing what she knows and writing the paper she wants to write, even though she realizes it will make her English teacher angry. "I see things from a lot of points of view," Anna says, and calling her ability to see from different viewpoints "creative" now rather than "crazy," she tells the following story.

The class was asked to write a hero legend, but Anna did not see this hero in the way her teacher did: "There was a la-dee-dah hero who went and saved all humankind." Anna explains:

If you see this hero from a different standpoint, from a different standpoint everyone could be a hero. So I wanted to write it from a Nazi standpoint, like Hitler as hero, and she really did not go for that at all. And I started to write, and she got really mad, and she was like, "I'm afraid you are going to come out sounding like a little Nazi."

Anna's solution was to write two papers, two versions of a hero legend: "a la-dee-dah legend and the one I wanted to write." She turned in both papers along with a letter to her teacher explaining her reasons. "She gave me an A on the normal one. I gave her the other one because I just had to write it. It sort of made me mad."

Anna wrote about Hitler "from the point of view of a little boy who was joining one of those groups that they had, and he was so proud to have a uniform and he went to try to salute . . . It did not come out about Hitler as much as about the reasons for Hitler," which interested Anna who was part German and whose father had been unemployed. Having watched her father and her brother resort to "brute force" in the face of frustration, Anna came to see how the need to appear heroic could lead men to cover vulnerability with violence. Viewed in this light, the hero legend became, in her eyes, an understandable but dangerous legend.

In choosing to disagree openly with her teacher and, in Woolf's terms, not to betray her mind or commit adultery of the brain, Anna said she was "just really mad." She regarded her teacher as "narrow-minded" in her insistence that Hitler was an "anti-hero" rather than a hero. "It was an urge," Anna says. "I had to write that paper because I was so mad . . . I had to write it to explain it to her, you know; I just had to . . . I just had to make her understand."

This urgent need to "make her understand," the overwhelming desire to connect with another person by bringing an honest voice into dialogue with their position, feels very pressing to girls who fight for authentic relationship and resist being shut up, put down, turned away, ignored. Anna's friend went to talk with the teacher on Anna's behalf; her mother encouraged her to write the paper but to do so in a way that would not antagonize the teacher. In the end, Anna concludes that her teacher "probably saw it as more annoying than anything else." What she learned from this experience, she said, "was not to antagonize people," her mother's caution. In fact, she was able both to speak and not antagonize people—in part, she suspects, because she had not been heard, because her teacher did not understand, but also because her teacher, however annoyed, was willing to listen and read both papers.

At fourteen, Anna sees the framework of the worlds she lives in. Painfully, she has become aware of the inconsistencies in the school's position on economic differences—where money is available and where it is not, the limits of the meritocracy it espouses. And seeing the inconsistencies, she becomes riveted by the disparity between what things are called and the realities, and she plays with the provocation of being literal in an effort to call things by their right names.

A year later, at fifteen, Anna begins to ask some literal questions about the order that is unquestioned in the world around her—questions about religion and about violence. She discovers that her questions are not welcomed by many of her classmates and her opinions are often met with silence; in the midst of a hotly controversial classroom conversation, she notices who is not speaking: "there were a bunch of people who just sat there like stones and listened."

In a diary entry that she suppresses, Anne Frank comments on the silences that surround the subject of sex. On March 18, 1944, at age fourteen, she observes that:

> Parents and people in general are very strange when it comes to [sexual matters]. Instead of telling their daughters as well as their sons everything when they are 12 years old, they send the children out of the room during such conversations and leave them to find things out for themselves. If the parents notice later on that the children have learned things anyway, then they assume that the children know either more or less than they actually do ... Grownups do come up against an important obstacle, although I'm sure that the obstacle is no more than a very small barrier, they believe that children will stop looking on marriage as something sacred and pure, when it dawns on them that in most cases the purity is nothing more than eyewash. (p. 545)

Like Anne Frank, Anna notes the readiness of adults to wash over what they do not want children to see—so that children, especially as they reach adolescence, are encouraged tacitly not to look at what they see or listen to what they hear, but to see everything as "nice." What puzzles Anna is the reluctance of people to speak about cruelty and violence. And yet she is also bothered when her mother refuses to conceal the realities of her life, and she is confused by what she is taking in—in part because of the disparity between what women are saying in the two worlds she lives in.

The acuity of Anna's perception is striking, and her descriptions of life in her family match Glen Elder and Avshalom Caspi's depiction of families living under economic hardship where fathers are unemployed and emotionally volatile and mothers and daughters bond. Anna's family constellation (herself and younger brothers) fits the picture for maximal psychological risk in children, given the finding that when families are under stress, the children most psychologically in danger are boys in early childhood and girls at adolescence. Anna's relationship with her mother appears crucial to Anna's resilience. Her closeness with her mother and the openness of their conversations are sometimes painful. Anna feels her mother's feelings "gnawing" at her. And it is sometimes confusing for Anna to know how her mother thinks and feels. She realizes that her mother's is "only one viewpoint" and she does not "know how much of it is dramatized." Yet she "can see that a lot of what my Mom says is true."

"You can't see someone like my Dad," she says, as an eleventh grader in the fifth year of the study, "without realizing how easily people are taken in." At school, she has "gotten a glimpse" behind the scenes and seen women whom she thought of as nice and compassionate "give away their color," after which, she observes, "all you can see is that part." "It is awful," she says, despairing at the capacity of people to cover over reality, the chameleon-like way her father changes his voice when, in the midst of screaming and yelling and ranting and raving at everyone in our house, the phone rings: "Hello"—like that. And it is really awful. Everyone thinks he is the strongest person, and when you see the other side, you just get so annoyed when people do that.

"I could," Anna muses, "probably give *the* best senior speech in the world in terms of shocking people, but people just don't, you know, it is so different, because there is just no one," she says with adolescent fervor, "no one who has to deal with anywhere near the same thing [as I do]." The violent outbursts of her father toward her brothers have brought social service agencies to the house; her brother's violence toward her mother has brought the police. Because of the social class difference, Anna may think hers is the only family (in her school) where violence happens. And yet she concludes, "Pollyanna"—that epitome of the nice girl—"would have problems . . . Thinking that life is peaches and cream is not realistic. It's not real . . . It really grates on you when you have someone around you who is like Pollyanna . . . that is really scary, you know; you can't deal with someone that like." The niceness that governs and sustains the school she attends cannot admit a world that she knows from experience . . . and Anna knows it. They are, she says, "totally different outlooks on life."

In the real world, Anna begins, "I have a bunch of friends that I talk to, and, you know, they understand and everything, but it is not very many people. This school," she concludes, "is not the real world." Anna, who loves school, who wants to take everything there is to take, to know everything she can know about the world—to learn Chinese and Latin as well as French and English—does not know how to imagine her future: whether she will enter the world that the people in her school think of as "normal"—the world reflected in its norms—or whether she will join Woolf's "Outsiders' Society" and, armed with an independent income to support her independent opinions, "be one of those people who go through college and get a Ph.D., and I'll live at the bottom of a mountain in Montana. Just one of those weird people. Have a chicken farm. I don't know. Then I will just write books or something," remaining outside, as Woolf envisioned, and experimenting "not with public means in public but with private means in private" (*Three Guineas*, p. 134).

IV. Perfect girls and dissidents

"The anxious bird," Jorie Graham writes in her poem "The Age of Reason,"

> . . . in the wild
>   spring green
> is *anting*, which means,
>   in my orchard
> he has opened his wings
>   over a furious
>
> anthill and will take up
>   into the delicate
> ridges of quince-yellow
>   feathers
> a number of tiny, angry
>   creatures

that will inhabit him, bewildered
   no doubt,
traveling deep
   into the air
on this feathery planet,
   new life—.

We don't know why
   they do it.
At times they'll take on
   almost anything
that burns, spreading
   their wings

over coals, over cigarette
   butts,
even, mistakenly, on bits
   of broken glass.
Meanwhile the light keeps
   stroking them

   as if it were love.

The poem is an inquiry about love. Love means open-ing; it means taking in. And Graham asks the question: what, in the name of love, is taken in? The world of nature, with its reminders of death—"The garden / continues its work / all round them, the gradual / openings that stand / for death" —and the world humans cultivate, the stories that grow in the hot-house of culture: "Under the plastic / groundcover the human / garden grows: help-sticks / and knots, row / after row. Who wouldn't want / to take / into the self / something that burns / or cuts, or wanders / lost / over the body?"

Who would, or wouldn't, in the name of love, take in films like Werner Herzog's *Woyzeck*, where,

> after the hero whom
>   we love
> who is mad has
>   murdered
>
> the world, the young
>   woman
> who is his wife,
>   and loved her,
> and covered himself
>   with blood,
>
> he grows frightened
>   by how quickly
> she softens and takes on the shape
>   of the soil

The emphasized lines, the short lines of this poem, in their staccato insistence, flash a warning to women, as when Emilia tries to warn Desdemona in the scene just before Othello murders her—tries to tell Desdemona before it is too late what she needs to know about men. Graham's words capture the essence of that warning, like nautical flags flying or newspaper headlines: *murdered / woman / and loved her / with blood.* How often, how far do we take this truth in? How do philosophers reason about this? What are reasonable answers to the poet's questions: "How far is true / enough? / How far into the earth / can vision go and / still be / love?"

At the end of November, when eleven-year-old Tessie is asked: "Looking back over the past year, what stays with you?" she says, "the summer, things that we do in the summer . . . like the sailing that we do and all the fun that I had going swimming and doing different things." Asked how she would describe herself to herself, Tessie says simply, "I like myself." Pleasure runs through Tessie's life like water flowing, swirling around her friends in the summer, her fights with her brother, swimming, reading, writing stories, her closeness with her mother, her special relationship with her father who "always wanted a daughter," along with her confidence and satisfaction in taking care of children, throwing sawdust on a classmate who made her angry, deciding it was worth it to get into trouble, helping people with difficult things or problems, meeting new people—"that's fun, you get to know more people as you go on."

But in the name of love, Tessie has also taken in an image of perfection, exemplified by her grandmother, a person she says she admires:

> She is *always* smiling and *always* laughing. She's *always* doing something helpful. I don't know. She goes to a nursing home, and she writes letters for people who can't write letters . . . She *always* has things made and *always* has things for little kids . . . She makes big terrariums and everything that she sells at the church fair, and she enjoys what she is doing, she loves her grandchildren and her children. And she seems to be an *always* happy person and *always* willing to help you and everything. (emphasis added)

The repeated word "always" catches the stillness at the center of this frozen image; Tessie's free-flowing world has suddenly stopped.

Ellen, also asked at eleven whether there is someone whom she admires, describes a variant of this image—a perfect girl who seems an offshoot of the always good woman, and the repeated word "really" suggests that Ellen may question if what she is seeing is real:

> There's this girl in our class who is perfect ... She's *really* tall, not *really* tall, she's tall and is pretty and she's good at everything. You could say something, and she could do it perfectly. And she's smart, and she is good at any sport, and she's good at art, and she's good at everything. She's like a person I know, like my mother's friend in college. She's good at everything. There is not one thing she cannot do. She's *really* nice and she's *always* being herself.

Claudia, the astute nine-year-old in Toni Morrison's *The Bluest Eye*, describes "this disrupter of seasons," the girl who entered the late elementary school classroom and "enchanted the entire school."

The ubiquity of this girl, her regular appearance at the threshold of adolescence in girls' lives and women's novels, signals a shift in the framework that alters what girls can and cannot see. Suddenly they are confronted with the incredible: a girl who is always nice, always generous, who has only good feelings and is good at everything. They find themselves judged against this model of perfection, which, because embodied, calls into question a reality they had taken for granted—the moving, changing reality of relationships and people. Mesmerized by the presence of this "perfect" girl, girls have entered the world of the hero legend. A framework

144

that seems to have come out of nowhere is suddenly everywhere. With the arrival of the perfect girl who exemplifies the incredible, girls are in danger of losing their world. But they are also in danger, in the world of the hero legend, if they continue to know what they know, and especially if they say it in public. What once seemed ordinary to girls—speaking, difference, anger, conflict, love and fighting, bad as well as good thoughts and feelings—now seems treacherous: laced with danger, a mark of imperfection, a harbinger of being left out, not chosen.

Like the hero or the superheroes of boys' early childhood, the perfect girl of girls' early adolescence is an emblem of loss. She embodies an idealization that covers a sadness that seems endless. In the presence of this emblem of perfection, woman and girls are pressed to silence an honest voice and to hide parts of themselves. Wanting her diary to be chosen for the Museum, Anne Frank removes the evidence of her desire to see for herself what she "looks like down there," she reduces the emotional complexity of her relationship with her mother, and she tones down her knowledge of the world and its values—moves sustained by her father, who then added a few edits of his own. In the edited diary—the one she intended for the Museum and prepared by her father for publication—Anne's anger toward her mother is not modulated. Taken by itself, it exemplifies what is considered normal between teenage girls and their mothers, the anger that facilitates separation. But in the actual diary, we see a far more complex struggle. It's not separation from her mother; it's actually that Anne is deeply connected to her mother, and both

145

pained by what she picks up and angry that her mother doesn't want her to see it.

In a diary passage her father removes and goes to great lengths to conceal, Anne expresses her admiration for her mother. On one of the days of their confinement, her father had told her that he had married her mother because "he deemed her the right person to be his wife." Anne writes, "I must say that I admire my mother for the way she has filled that position without a murmur and without jealousy, as far as I can tell . . . Father is not in love, he gives her a kiss the way he kisses us" (February 8, 1944). As for her mother,

> Quite possibly because of her great sacrifice Mother has grown hard and disagreeable toward her surroundings and consequently, she will drift further and further away from the path of love, will gain less and less admiration and, no doubt, Father will eventually come to realize that because externally she has never claimed his full love, she has crumbled away bit by bit internally. She loves him more than anybody else and it is hard to see this kind of love unanswered time and again. (February 8, 1944, deleted from the Critical Edition at the request of the Frank family, quoted by Ralph Blumenthal, "Five Precious Pages Renew Wrangling over Anne Frank." *New York Times*, September 10, 1998.)

Her insight is stunning. It combines a child's sensibility with the razor-sharp intelligence of adolescence. Her father had recounted his tragic love story (he had been in love with another woman before meeting Anne's mother but her parents had ruled out a marriage on financial grounds). But Anne is gripped less by his tragic story than by the cost of the sacrifice her mother has made. It is a sacrifice she rejects for herself, and in doing so, she identifies herself as a resister. Her ability, even fleetingly, to see her mother as a complete person—as another woman rather than the other woman—brings to the fore our difficulty in hearing a story about women that does not pit them in competition. It is a story her father does not want us to hear, in part because Anne is not seeing it from his viewpoint. He is willing to make public Anne's anger at her mother, but not her understanding of the reasons for the emotional distance she struggles against repeatedly, or her insight into her mother's predicament: "For a woman in love it cannot be easy to know that she will never occupy the first place in her husband's heart, and Mother knew" (February 8, 1944).

Wanting her diary to be chosen by fathers for inclusion in their War Museum, Anne Frank hides those aspects of herself that she anticipates would lead them to dismiss her as "insufferable" or "unpleasant." Assuming a mask of innocence, a kind of psychological virginity, she—who knew so much—presents herself as knowing less than she knew. The evidence she covered reveals her connection with her body, with her own desire, with her mother, and with the world in which she was living—a world that contains both the story of *Woyzeck* and the Nazis. Living in the midst of real terror, she had not lost her sense of reality.

If girls' knowledge of reality is politically dangerous, it is both psychologically and politically dangerous for girls not to know what is going on—or to render themselves innocent by disconnecting themselves from their bodies, that repository of experience and desire, and

147

thus, in effect, dissociating themselves from themselves, from relationships, and from what they know to be true. Because girls are encouraged to make these disconnections at the time of their adolescence, their dissent at this time becomes psychologically essential. And their resistance can be healing for boys as well. At adolescence, girls' knowledge and girls' passion are bound to make trouble in the world they are entering.

When Rosie is interviewed at age fourteen, her vitality is infectious. In the privacy of the interview setting, she speaks openly about desire as sexual—in somewhat the same tentative yet resolute manner that Anne Frank describes in preparing to speak about her body ("When the subject [of what a naked girl looks like] comes up again, how in heaven's name will you be able to explain what things are like [down there] without using examples? Shall I try it out here in the meantime? Well then get on with it!" [p. 567]). Yet Rosie is in trouble at school for her outspokenness, her irreverence, and her refusal, despite her evident brightness, to be the perfect student.

At fifteen, Rosie and her boyfriend are caught in the park by a ranger who calls her mother to come and take Rosie home. Rosie was embarrassed and scared about what was going to happen to her and also worried about disillusioning her mother who "had this image of me . . . as close to the perfect child." When I ask her to describe this perfect child, she says without hesitation: "She gets straight As and has a social life, but still gets home exactly on the dot, on time, and does everything her parents say, and keeps her room neat." I ask Rosie,

"Are there girls like this?" She says, "Perhaps; saints."
"Do saints have sex?" I wonder, thinking of Rosie. "I
don't know," she begins, and then fills in what had been
her solution: "If they want, as long as they don't get
caught; as long as nobody knows."

Once her mother knows, Rosie "hunted her down
and . . . made her talk to me. And it wasn't like a battle
or anything . . . I just wanted to talk to her and see
what she had to say." Like Anna who wants to connect her own with her teacher's view of the hero legend,
Rosie wants to discover what connections are possible
between herself and her mother, what her mother is
willing to say.

Rosie's clarity, her playfulness, her irreverence in
refusing to disembody saints, and her courage in staying in her own body coexist with confusion about the
world she lives in. Despite her efforts, she cannot find
the emotional center—the place where desire and pleasure live in her mother's busy life. From her mother, she
takes in the caution that she must be more careful about
her body, more attentive to the warning signals and
the flags of danger. Perhaps the seemingly disembodied
perfect girl whom her mothers and teachers envision
she could be really exists and is admirable, exemplifying
how Rosie should live in order to take care of herself in
a world where imperfection often means rejection and
where, more darkly, sex can be fatal, love can mean
murder, and fighting can mean violence.

At the end of *Oedipus Tyrannus*, that psychologically
astute telling of the hero legend, after the truth has been
uncovered and Oedipus learns that it was his mother

who gave him to the shepherd, Oedipus blinds himself, Jocasta strangles herself, their sons run off to become kings and war with one another, and their daughters are summoned by their father to accompany him in his blindness. It is tempting to see this as a *tableau vivant* of life in the patriarchal family, showing how the wounds fathers suffer in early childhood afflict their daughters in adolescence. In a play filled with riddles and questions, the chorus puzzles over Jocasta's silence: "How could the Queen whom Laius won, / Be silent when that deed was done?"

V. Women teaching girls / Girls teaching women

It is September, and the sky over New England is Fra Angelico blue. I am flying to Cleveland to talk with the teachers at the Laurel School about our research with the girls they are teaching. It is the beginning of the second year of the project, and the library fills as I enter, the faculty sitting in rows crossing the room with a long aisle running down the center. School—the microcosm in children's lives of the public world, the public space that Hannah Arendt saw as the crucible of democracy, the place where the natality and plurality, the ever new and always different nature of the human condition, can flourish.

The school is governed by an honor code for which everyone is responsible. In the privacy of the research interview, girls spoke about the honor code from a different angle, as giving rise to dilemmas of relationship: how to honor the code and also stay in relationship with other girls. They saw no way to bring up these conflicts in the public arena of the school without exposing themselves to moral condemnation. Hence, many girls voted for an honor code they did not honor or believe in. But they also took matters of governance—the maintenance of trust and public safety—into their own hands and settled them in private, drawing on their psychological knowledge to resolve intricate problems of relationships.

Like a perfectly run household, this girls' school was being maintained as if effortlessly. In reality, it was governed by an underground society of girls.

I decide to focus my presentation to the teachers on these questions: Why are girls voting for an honor code they do not believe in? Why aren't they bringing their activities on behalf of the school into the public arena?

Standing in the library, with teachers and administrators arrayed before me, I register the atmosphere of decorum; like the books on the shelves, everything is in order. I take a deep breath and begin. I describe the research and what we heard in our initial interviews about the moral conflicts posed by the honor code and the choices girls made. The teachers listen attentively; I cannot read their faces. I then go on to observe that in educating girls to become citizens in a democratic society, it is important for them to learn how to voice their disagreements in public.

In the front row to my right, a woman—small-boned, white hair, intense face concentrating energy as her thoughts and feelings connect with sound and come out into the air of the room on her voice—says: "How can we help girls learn to deal with disagreement in public, when we"—she looks across the rows, quickly

151

scanning the faces of her colleagues, women and men—
"when we," meaning now women, "cannot deal with
disagreement in public ourselves?"

Silence washes over the room. The research had
exposed what goes on beneath the surface. Girls' voices,
recorded in private and amplified in the public space of
the school, resonated with women teachers, encouraging them to ask themselves: what were they teaching
girls about relationships, about speaking, about conflict,
about disagreement, about psychological and political
resistance?

At the lunch that follows, women teachers approach
me. I hear about migraine headaches, digestive ail-
ments. They express a wish to talk further about the
issues raised by the research. Why don't we go on
retreat together, one woman suggests, meaning the
teachers and the research team. And so, the Women
teaching girls / Girls teaching women retreats begin, first
with women teachers (spanning primary and secondary grades) and administrators at the Laurel School in
Cleveland, and subsequently with women middle school
teachers and principals in the Boston public schools. Led
by members of the research team, the retreats are framed
by two questions: As a woman teaching girls, where do I
stand in relation to the knowledge I am passing along to
the next generation; what do I think it is important for
girls to know? And, where am I, a woman who was once
a girl, in relation to girls, the next generation of women?

Are women simply vessels through which the culture
passes? Are women oracles of the disciplines, con-
veying like the oracle of Apollo the wisdom of male
gods? Provocative questions. But it was the relationship

between girls and women that proved transformative, and more specifically, women's relationships with girls who were entering womanhood.

Education is the nonviolent means of social change, an alternative to revolution. But it is also the way the norms of society are reinforced again and again. And primary and secondary education in the U.S., for a variety of good and bad reasons, is largely in the hands of women who as mothers, teachers, and therapists are in direct contact with children's desires for love and for knowledge, and also in touch with their resistance.

The question stirs: what if women. . . ? irrepressible question! Half the population in every generation. Could women, as Madeline Grumet envisions, turn the practice of teaching from "women's work" into "the work of women," so that instead of what Grumet calls "the great escape" from the daily rhythms of the maternal order to the clock time of the paternal state, women would constitute a new order (using private means in private as Woolf would have it) by finding new words and creating new methods?

At the beginning of Act Two of *Lysistrata*, Lysistrata despairs: the women are leaving the Acropolis and rushing home to their husbands. "I know you miss your husbands," she says, "but don't you realize that they miss you as well? . . . Be strong sisters," she enjoins them: "There is an oracle that we will triumph if only we don't fall out among ourselves."

The moral philosopher Sara Ruddick heals what is perhaps the major division within and among women— the division between mother and resister—by defining a politics of resistance that is relationally rather than

153

heroically conceived. This practice is rooted in the body (its vulnerability, its promise, its power); it is a practice of "preservative love." Taking her cue from the Madres of Argentina and the women of Chile, she lays out a strategy of resistance that draws its imperative from the singularity of human beings and the irreplaceability of human relationships, rather than from visions of immortality and superhuman strength. If only women would make a shift within their practice of motherhood, separating out those elements that support militarism (the worshipping of martyrs and heroes) from those which subvert it (women's irreverent language of loyalty, love, and outrage), women could move readily, Ruddick suspects, "from denial to truthfulness, from parochialism to solidarity, from inauthenticity to active responsibility" (*Maternal Thinking*, pp. 227–30). In short, women could move from psychological to political resistance.

Central to this journey is the recovery of anger as the bellwether of oppression, injustice, bad treatment; the signal that something is wrong in the relational surround (a fin on the horizon, a dark shadow). Writing about women and anger from the two-culture vantage point of an Argentinean-born, American psychoanalyst, Teresa Bernardez reminds her reader that cultural injunctions against anger in women turn into psychological inhibitions that "prevent rebellious acts," with the result that women come to feel complicit in their own misery. Resistance then involves a kind of reverse alchemy whereby anger that has soured into bitterness or hatred becomes once again simply anger—"the conscious response to an awareness of injustices suffered or losses and grievances sustained . . . [the anger] which involves self-love and awareness of responsibility for making choices" ("Woman and Anger," p. 5). Like eleven-year-old Sarah's anger that lives in the daylight of her relationships, or Tessie's anger which sits comfortably side-by-side with love. Bernardez notes that when people are living under conditions of political oppression or terror, they often come not to know what they know and "have forgotten what they have forgotten." She also observes that anger silenced "contributes to the making of depression." And depression in women tends to begin in adolescence.

Perhaps women have forgotten girls. And not remembered their own disconnections at adolescence—the losses they suffered, the injuries sustained. So that relationships between adolescent girls and women hold a key to the psychology and politics of resistance.

When Anjli brought her paper on "To His Coy Mistress" to her English teacher, Mrs. Franklin, Nancy Franklin realized she was hearing the poem in a way she had not heard it before—very differently from the way she had learned to interpret it in the course of her graduate training. Anjli was taking an advanced English class taught simultaneously at several schools in the Cleveland area; the assignment was to analyze the poem for tone. Nancy Franklin was one of the women in the Women teaching girls / Girls teaching women retreats. As such, she was among the women pursuing the question: what does it mean to be a woman teaching girls? And in the setting of the retreat, in the third year of our meeting, she speaks of her decision to join Anjli's resistance.

Listening for the tone of Andrew Marvell's poem in her house late at night, Anjli suddenly began writing in the first person to record what she was hearing: the voice of an older man bent on overcoming a young woman's resistance ("Had we but world enough, and time / This coyness, Lady, were no crime"). Reading Anjli's paper, Nancy Franklin was struck anew by the power of Marvell's poem. In the retreat, she recalls Anjli's voice for the group:

> I am writing this paper and it is late at night, and I am terrified because this is such a morbid poem ("Thy beauty shall no more be found, / Nor, in thy marble vault, shall sound / My echoing song: then worms shall try / That long preserved virginity, / And your quaint honor turn to dust, / And into ashes all my lust."). This is such a frightening poem.

Anjli's paper was submitted to six teachers in a cross-grading exercise, designed to ensure consistency of standards. Franklin recalls that one woman wrote on the paper: "She doesn't understand *carpe diem*. Why doesn't she know this term? This is not a college level paper." Another wrote, "She misreads Marvell's playfulness." And yet—Nancy Franklin says, caught momentarily by the standards of her colleagues in English and then resisting their disconnection from Anjli, their dismissal of her reading—"this paper was beautiful, and it made me see the poem in a new way." Sustaining this connection, she draws out its implications for Anjli, for herself, and for the educational system.

> This is a young girl; this is a seventeen-year-old, very innocent but very bright girl. Reading this, Lord knows,

you go back and read that poem at two o'clock in the morning. And she was terrified—the voice of an older man speaking to a young girl. And the comments she got on this paper. They all said: C—you know, no good. "Doesn't know stanzaic patterns, missed all this playfulness, and *carpe diem, carpe diem.*" Now there's an educational system at work. What did it tell her? Go underground; to survive, go underground, at least until you get out of this system. Or worse.

Anjli read the graders' comments, discussed them with her teacher, remembered hearing about *carpe diem*, reread the poem, and Franklin writes, "found that indeed she could see the poem that way, but more importantly, she could see it both ways." She knows that "she could rewrite the paper now that she understands the way she was supposed to react, saying what she is supposed to say. . . . 'If you were a guy,' she says, smiling, 'it might be really funny'." But Anjli cringes at the poem's morbid images: "I don't think a class full of girls could really laugh at this." What is puzzling then, given Anjli's perspective, and also potentially treacherous, is the position of the women graders. Anjli assumes that she will be understood by girls, but she cannot assume such understanding from women.

At the intersection between political resistance and psychological resistance, at the time of adolescence, girls' psychological development becomes indelibly political. If girls know what they know and bring their honest voices into their work, they will find themselves in conflict with those in positions of power. If they override what they know and silence an honest response, they will be in trouble with themselves. The ability of girls to tell it from both sides and to see it both ways is not an indication of relativism or a post-modern sensibility—or not only that; it is a demonstration of girls' understanding of relationship raised to a cultural level and a provisional solution to a difficult problem of relationship: how to stay connected with themselves and with others, how to keep in touch with themselves and with the world around them.

As eleven-year-old Tessie underscores the importance of voicing her argument with her mother so she can hear both sides, so Anjli voices the disparity between how she reacts and how she is supposed to react, what she says and what she is supposed to say, according to the authorities who correct and grade her. And Tessie's openness, at least in theory, to her friend's hearing her mother's voice differently from the way she does, corresponds to Anjli's generosity toward those who hear the poem differently: the guys (whom she thought might find it funny) and the graders. Women teaching girls, then, are faced with intricate dilemmas of relationship. Girls must learn the traditions that frame the world they are entering but they must also hold onto their own ways of hearing and seeing if they are to do original and creative work. How can women stay with girls and also teach cultural traditions? How can girls stay with women and also with themselves? What can women teach girls about living in a world that still, in the twenty-first century, is largely governed by men?

"What happens to girls when they get to that age?" Sharon Miller asks, turning to the women around her. She is asking about the riddle of girls' development:

why is it that girls who seem more intelligent and livelier than boys of the same age, who go out more to meet the external world and at the same time form stronger connections with people, often become less intelligent and lively when they reach adolescence? Like girls in novels and poems written by women, girls interviewed in contemporary school settings speak about taking themselves out of relationships as they approach adolescence, "building a little shield," "getting afraid to say when you're mad at somebody," "losing confidence in myself." Taking their honest voices out of their relationships, they are self-consciously letting go of themselves.

What happens to girls when they reach this age? "I think," Sharon Miller says, "they have let go of themselves. I think it is the unusual middle school girl who can say, 'if you don't like me the way I am, fine!' Most girls can't say that because there is no one there." Why not? I ask her. I am thinking of girls who are so resolute, so present at eleven. "Well that's the question," Miller responds. "You know, what happens to girls when they get to that age? Well, because that is the age when girls start identifying with adult women."

And then suddenly, seeing the circle closing, Miller says, hand rising, covering her mouth, "My God," as tears begin flowing, "And there is nothing there."

Like a film running backwards, women teaching girls arrive at the moments of their own resistance and come up against their own solutions to the problems of relationships girls face. Then women may encounter their own reluctance to know what they know and come to the realization that this knowledge is contained in their body; they may discover that they have succumbed to the temptation to model perfection by trying to be perfect role-models for girls and thus have taken themselves out of relationship with girls— in part to hide their imperfections but also perhaps to shield girls from their sadness and their anger. Women teaching girls, however, also may discover that they are harboring within themselves a girl who lives in her body, who is insistent on speaking, who intensely desires relationships and knowledge, and who, perhaps at the time of adolescence, went underground or was overwhelmed.

Girls have picked up this hidden woman. They are looking for her in women, sensing her absence or her silent presence. And although women, in the name of being good women, may have been modeling for girls her repudiation, teaching girls the necessity of a loss or renunciation that girls question, girls are teaching women to question their silences. Through girls, then, women can find or strengthen their honest voices and their courage.

There is evidence now of a new cycle beginning, breaking up an old impasse in women's development and affecting men as well. If women and girls stay with one another at the time when girls reach adolescence, girls' playfulness and irreverence will tap the wellsprings of women's resistance. And women in turn, taking in girls' embodiment, their outspokenness and their courage, will join girls in their desire for relationship and for knowledge and, by doing so, teach girls that they can say what they want and know without being left all alone.

Coda

"Dear Kitty," Anne Frank writes on January 6, 1944 at the age of fourteen, in a passage from her diary that her father edited:

> I have three things to confess to you today ... I <u>must</u> tell someone, and you are the best to tell, as I know that come what may you always keep a secret ... You know that I've grumbled a lot about Mummy, yet still tried to be nice to her again. Now it's suddenly clear to me what she lacks. Mummy herself has told us that she looked upon us more as her friends than her daughters; now that is all very fine of course, but still a friend can't take a mother's place. *I need my mother as an example which I can follow. I want to be able to respect her and though my mother is an example to me in most things she is precisely the kind of example that I do not want to follow.* I have the feeling that Margot [Anne's sister] thinks differently about these things and would never be able to understand what I've just told you. And Daddy avoids all arguments about Mummy. (The italicized lines are those Anne's father deleted) (p. 440)

"<u>One Conclusion</u>," Emma writes, beginning a new page in her journal:

> One of the conclusions I come to is that many/most of the paintings/statues/artwork of women I have seen are of women naked. A lot of the art of women that I saw was done by men. Maybe because the women posed. None of the girls I saw were naked. Maybe because artists like to have people pose naked, and they think women are better because they have more growth.

"One question," Malka writes at the end of her second conversation with the Queen of Babylon: "Did these people, places, painted, sculpted, did they live? Did they live in the heart of the painter, sculptor?"

"Wouldn't there have been," Anna says irreverently—she has just finished writing a paper on the church and Galileo—"Wouldn't there have been a lot of animal stuff on Noah's ark after forty days?"

"I think I am trying," Rosie says, " to attach value to things. This is important. This is not important. Maybe order things more." "What do you order them to?" I ask, wondering what key she is tuning to, what standard she has in mind. And Rosie, the embodied saint, the underground woman, suddenly turns philosophical: "I don't know . . . but I guess I know that there should be an order, and I was trying to decide what that order was. Maybe that is part of what I am looking for . . . an order to my life. This is getting deep, philosophical."

I am listening to girls' questions—following girls' inquiry into relationships as it becomes more philosophical, more critical, and also more psychologically and politically dangerous. Emma's curiosity is edging toward men's feelings about women's bodies; Malka begins to trace the channels connecting men's hearts with cultural icons. If this inquiry continues, girls will find the line that connects the personal and the political, the line that extends from the psychology of men to the cultural framework of the world in which they are living. And they will wonder how they fit in.

"I don't know . . ." Rosie says. "I guess I know," she follows, in rapid succession. She is observing how her mother spends her life, her time, asking in essence the same question that Malka asked the Queen of Babylon: "Whatchya doing?" And seeing what her mother, a busy physician, has to say—whether her mother might come up with the Queen's funny answer: "Brushing my hair. I was interrupted this morning by news of a revolt," an answer that captures the doubling of women's lives and perceptions and speaks directly to girls' questions about what gives women pleasure and what women value.

Rosie, a sharp-eyed adolescent, notices that her mother's "small study and bedroom are messy." She will have to create her own order of living, find some way to orchestrate her life. "I don't know . . . I know . . . you know . . . do you know? . . ." Voices from the underground, speaking under the sign of repression, marking dissociations that are still tenuous, knowledge that is fragile, reaching out for connections that sustain the hope that a secret underground will become a public resistance. Then a healthy resistance, rather than turning inward and becoming corrosive, can stay in the open air of relationships. And by remaining political, work to bring a new order of living into the world.

5 Resisting Injustice: A Feminist Ethic of Care

Even in totalitarian societies that target the psyche for attack, there are always some people who see through the lies and speak truth to power. We think of them as heroic, which they are. Yet listening to women who took great risks under the Nazis—Magda Trocmé, the pastor's wife in Le Chambon-sur-Lignon who responded when Jews knocked at her door by saying "Come in"; Antonina Zabinska, the zookeeper's wife in occupied Warsaw, who hid Jews in the zoo in the center of the city—what they say, when asked how they came to do this, is that they were human. They did what any person would have done.

I am haunted by these women, their refusal of exceptionality. When asked how they did what they did, they say they were human, no more no less. What if we take them at their word? Then, rather than asking how do we gain the capacity to care, how do we develop a capacity for mutual understanding, how do we learn to take the point of view of the other or overcome the pursuit of self-interest, they prompt us to ask instead: how do we lose the capacity to care, what inhibits our ability to empathize with others, and most painfully, how do we lose the capacity to love? It is the absence of care or the failure to care that calls for explanation.

I am haunted too by the Christmas truce of 1914, a "human episode amid all the atrocities which have stained the memories of war," as Arthur Conan Doyle described it. In the fifth month of a fifty-two-month war, on Christmas Eve, British and German soldiers spontaneously stopped fighting. At the sight of candles on small trees strung along the German trenches and the sound of Christmas carols wafting back and forth across No Man's Land, the overlay of war dissolved. For twenty-four hours, soldiers exchanged small gifts— one Brit who loved buttons wrote home that a German had cut two buttons off his coat for him. They retrieved their dead; a soccer ball was kicked around. No man's land became everyman's land. This was not a myth, the BBC reminds us; it "really happened."

And so did the bullying stop, at least to a significant extent, when babies were brought into classrooms. A Canadian educator, Mary Gordon, had the idea and started the "Roots of Empathy" program in Toronto. Each month during the school year, three forty-minute visits were scheduled: a pre-visit, a baby visit, and a post-visit, led by a trained instructor. From kindergarten through seventh grade, a mother came with her baby (between two and four months at the beginning of the school year). David Bornstein reports:

> During the baby visits, the children sit around the baby and mother (sometimes it's a father) on a green blanket

(which represents new life and nature) and they try to understand the baby's feelings. The instructor helps by labeling them. "It's a launch pad for them to understand their own feelings and the feelings of others," explains Gordon. "It carries over to the rest of the class."

Observing these sessions, Bornstein was struck by "how the baby actually changes the children's behavior. Teachers have confirmed my impressions: tough kids smile, disruptive kids focus, shy kids open up. In a seventh grade class, I found 12-year-olds unabashedly singing nursery rhymes." The baby acts "like a heart-softening magnet," drawing to itself human qualities that seemingly had hardened.

As Bornstein reports, Roots of Empathy was evaluated in four studies by Kimberly Schonert-Reichl, a developmental psychologist and professor at the University of British Columbia. Asked if the kids became more empathic and understanding, less aggressive and kinder to one another, Professor Schonert-Reichl replied: "Yes and yes." The results were dramatic. When the project was taken to scale in Manitoba and instituted across the province in 300 classrooms, the proportion of children who got into fights fell from 15 percent to 8 percent, close to a 50 percent reduction. The surprise was that the effects were lasting: "Outcomes are maintained or enhanced three years after the program ends."

How to explain the success of this inexpensive and uncluttered intervention? Gordon offers the following suggestion: "When you've got emotion and cognition happening at the same time, that's deep learning. That's learning that will last." A key may be that in each class, the children were enlisted to do something to care for the baby, something that established an emotional connection: singing a song, speaking in a gentle voice, or making a "wishing tree" (an object for wishes and offerings). "Empathy can't be taught," Gordon says, "but it can be caught." To her, the biggest surprise was that empathy increased not only in the children but also in their teachers.

However mythic or exceptional these instances may appear in a world of "dog eat dog" (an improbable occurrence), they sound a common theme. Underneath the terror, the war, the bullying, there is a human face. And voice, however suppressed. In 2010, when for the first time the International Psychoanalytical Association met in Asia, in Beijing, Chinese analysts reported their experience. As in nineteenth-century Vienna, free association released voices that had been bottled up. Reporting for the *New York Times*, Didi Tatlow reminds us that psychoanalysis had been banned by the Communist Party for decades after the 1949 revolution, dismissed as bourgeois superstition (sports and revolutionary ardor were recommended for mental health). Permitted only in the past twenty years, it revealed that "violent political campaigns that killed tens of millions in the past and tight controls over freedom of expression that persist to this day, have left a significant legacy of trauma."

The story then is consistent: our brains are malleable, we are adaptable, but as humans we have a capacity for voice and resistance. I return then to the developmental narrative to add a crucial final chapter: Niobe Way's study of "boys' friendships and the crisis of connection." Way is a developmental psychologist, and she has been studying boys' friendships for over two decades. Titling her book *Deep Secrets*, she opens with the voice of Justin, a fifteen-year-old in an urban public school. Responding to a question about close friendships, Justin says:

> [My best friend and I] love each other . . . that's it . . . you have this thing that is deep, so deep, it's within you, you can't explain it. It's just a thing that you know that that person is that person . . . and that is all that should be important in our friendship . . . I guess in life, sometimes two people can really, really understand each other and really have a trust, respect, and love for each other. It just happens, it's human nature. (p. 1)

Echoing the voices of women resisters, Justin speaks about human nature, our capacity to "really understand each other and really have a trust, respect, and love for each other." As he says, it "is deep, so deep, it's within you, you can't explain it," but it's something you know. Something that "just happens."

But something else "just happens" that Justin describes two years later, as a high school senior. Asked how his friendships have changed since he was a freshman, he says:

> I don't know, maybe not a lot, but I guess that best friends become close friends. So that's basically the only thing that changed. It's like best friends become close friends, close friends become general friends, and then general friends become acquaintances. So they just . . . If there's distance, whether it's I don't know, natural or whatever. You can say that but it just happens that way. (p. 19)

168

Justin doesn't know if this distance is "natural," but by the end of high school, he is among the majority of the boys in Way's studies who "spoke about having and wanting intimate male friendships and then gradually losing these relationships and their trust in their male peers" (p. 12). As Joseph, another boy, explains: "You can't trust nobody these days." Guillermo, asked in his junior year if he has a close or best friend, says, "Not really. I think myself. The friend I had, I lost." And Mohammed, who as a freshman and sophomore had spoken of telling his best friend all his secrets, says when interviewed as a junior, "I don't know. Recently . . . you know I kind of changed something. Not that much, but you know I feel like there's no need to—I could keep [my feelings] to myself. You know, I'm mature enough."

As Way reveals, boys know the value of close friendships. They tell her and her team of interviewers this directly. As a high school junior, George says that without a best friend, meaning someone you can tell your secrets to, you would "go whacko." At fifteen, Chen says that without a close friend "you go crazy." Others speak of how anger builds up inside them when they don't have a best friend to talk to. Some speak about sadness, loneliness, and depression. Asked what he likes about his best friend, Felix, a sophomore, says, "regardless of what happens, he will be there." But while boys will describe their loss of best friendships and name the emotional costs (going whacko, becoming angry or sad), they nevertheless tend to dismiss the loss and downplay its consequences. Like Justin, they don't quite know if it's "natural or whatever." What they know is "it just happens."

Way's findings recall the qualities Judy Chu and I observed in younger boys—the "delight he has with his friends" that Michael found so striking in his four-year-old son. Kevin, a high school sophomore in Way's study, evokes the "spunk" and "real joy" that the fathers wanted to preserve in their four- and five-year-old boys when he says that what he likes about his close friends is "the energy, the energy. There is so much love between all of us."

Following the four- and five-year-olds from pre-kindergarten into kindergarten and first grade, Chu noticed them becoming more inattentive, more inarticulate, more indirect and inauthentic in their relationships with one another and with her. They were becoming "boys." With Jake, the eleven-year-old boy in *In a Different Voice*, I made the reverse observation. At eleven, Jake sounds like a "real boy" when he says that moral dilemmas are "sort of like a math problem with humans." He solves the Heinz dilemma on grounds of pure logic: Heinz should steal the drug to save his dying wife because the druggist "can get more money from rich people with cancer, but you can't get Heinz's wife again." We catch a glimpse of a more psychological understanding, but Jake holds to logic as he explains, "People are all different, so you couldn't get Heinz's wife again." At fifteen, however, when asked "Should Heinz steal the drug?" Jake interjects a question of his own: "You have to ask how a man would feel with his wife dying and him having to deal with her dying." The math problem has become a human story.

Entering "the hidden landscape of boys' friendships," Way discovers the depths of boys' capacities for love

170

and empathy, mutual understanding and care. Over and over again, across cultures and class, boys in baggy jeans or white shirts, with trim cuts or dreadlocks, speak of their love for their best friends. Yet Way finds that, by the end of high school, these same boys align masculinity with independence, they display emotional stoicism, and they hedge any depiction of closeness with other boys with the phrase "no homo."

Within themselves, boys know they are covering a truth. They read the culture around them, they see what they are doing, they resist at the same time as they reveal the power of the forces that beset them, the sting of being called a wimp or a sissy, being targeted as gay or seen as acting like a girl. Way asks us to look beyond the explanations commonly given for the drop in close male friendships. Boys will say that they "don't have time" for friends, and besides, by late adolescence they are "more interested in having a girlfriend (i.e., sex) than in having a male friend." Way calls these "thin culture explanations," in that they remain on the surface. They repeat stereotypes and clichés, accepting what happens as fact rather than asking, for example, why boys don't have time for friends, or why now there is a "boy crisis."

"Thick culture explanations" address these questions. They interrogate the culture itself (as revealed through stereotypes, clichés, etc.). They reject thin interpretations on the grounds that they render the culture invisible. As Way explains, they "[lead] us into the thick of it," drawing "attention to the ways in which conventions and the gender straitjackets associated with them have grown more rigid as we become more socially progressive, revealing a powerful backlash to women's and gay rights." They examine "the larger sociological pattern of a decline in social connectedness and empathy that most assuredly makes it difficult for boys to stay connected to each other." But in her analysis, the prime culprit is the set of assumptions about gender that keep us from "hearing what boys are saying about their friendships and point to our cultural equation of emotional vulnerability with being gay and girlish" (p. 26). To those who subscribe to this equation, researchers who expose boys' "deep secrets" appear to be promoting homosexuality or turning boys into girls.

In his junior year interview, George observes that some people try to "cover the sun with their hands," meaning, "they always try to hide the obvious truth." The obvious truth Way asks us to see is that boys are human. The question she raises is: why has it come to seem "natural or whatever" for boys to hide this?

Placing Way's research alongside the research with girls and the studies of four- and five-year-old boys, it becomes clear that human capacities are besieged or come under stress when children discover that in order to be one of the boys or to become a man, or to be one of the girls we want to be with (not one of those other girls) or to become a good woman, they must dissociate themselves from their humanity.

Taken together, these studies of boys' and girls' development highlight adolescence as a time of opportunity. Girls are resisting the loss of an honest voice and boys are regaining their desire for close friendships. The threshold of adulthood thus becomes a prime time for educating the capacity to care by demonstrating what it means to pay attention, teaching how to listen, and exploring different ways of responding and their ramifications. It is a time when erotic desire becomes more insistent, taking us into our bodies, and when the deepening of subjectivity enhances our capacity for emotional intimacy. And perhaps it is no accident that at precisely this moment, the Love Laws go into effect, enforcing who should be loved, and how, and how much.

When David Richards and I saw the convergence between the freeing of a voice that resists injustice and the freeing of a voice that resists the Love Laws, when we realized how often throughout history the repression of an ethically resisting voice was accompanied by a tightening of the Love Laws, a series of observations fell into place. We understood why the 1960s—a time of ethical resistance and constitutional advance—became tarred as an era of "sex, drugs, and rock 'n' roll." As if that's all there was to it, or as if the freeing of sexuality erased the progress made toward social justice. And even on the left, the outrage at President Clinton for his lies about his sexual behavior was several emotional decibels higher than the condemnation of President Bush for his lies about a war that has caused a hundred thousand deaths. As in the move from republic to empire in the Rome of Augustus, the conflicts between democracy and patriarchy are playing out right before our eyes. The politics of repression and the economics of inequality are reflected (if not drowned out) by a culture obsessed with the struggle between a licentious sexuality—a sexuality divorced from relationships—and

173

a puritanical hysteria: two poles within a framework of dissociation.

Way noted that in early adolescence boys resist the canons of patriarchal masculinity. Embracing love and mutual understanding, they break the gender binary. But she heard it return along with the hierarchy as boys reassumed a cloak of masculinity that Chu and I had seen younger boys put on literally as well as figuratively, dressing themselves in the garb of superheroes as they covered their tenderness, their vulnerability, their emotional sensitivity. "I don't know," girls will say as they bury an honest voice inside them; "I don't care," boys say as their relational desires become deep secrets.

There is no mystery here, just obfuscation. The role morality has played in dividing us from what we now recognize to be our humanity is one of the tragic stories of civilization.

Since the Holocaust, theories of moral development have been challenged by the recognition that the usual markers of development—intelligence and education—do not form a barrier against atrocity. In one sense, we have known this for a long time. Yet we continue to be surprised when injustice is perpetrated by "the best and the brightest," as David Halberstam described the men who led the U.S. into Vietnam.

For over ten years now, David Richards and I have been teaching a seminar on resisting injustice at New York University's school of law. We were impelled to teach together by a desire to join David's work on the history of ethical resistance within constitutional democracies and my research on psychological development in the hope that this joining might bring new light to the questions: Why does systemic injustice persist in societies committed to democratic institutions and values? and What are the wellsprings of ethical resistance?

Our exploration of these questions has led us to see the ethic of care, grounded in voice and relationship, as an ethic of resistance both to injustice and to self-silencing. It is a human ethic, integral to the practice of democracy and to the functioning of a global society. More controversially, it is a feminist ethic, an ethic that guides the historic struggle to free democracy from patriarchy.

"Do you consider yourself a feminist?" I am asked in the spring of 2009 by one of the women attending the twentieth reunion of the Harvard Women's Leadership Project. The project began in the late 1980s to educate and encourage women undergraduates who had shown a potential for leadership. The women attending the reunion thus range in age from those just graduated to those twenty years out. They gather in the informal, basement dining room of the Faculty Club for a discussion I was invited to lead. I look forward to hearing the concerns of these bright and educationally privileged young women, some dressed in business casual, some more informally in jeans and sweaters. Wedding rings gleam on many fingers, a few of the women are visibly pregnant. Yet I find my attention wandering as the discussion takes a predictable course: exceptional husbands are touted, children are celebrated, work is described. Until suddenly, a division slices the group. On one side are the women who work, on the other those who stay home with their children. The slice came with the accusation that the stay-at-home mothers were "not working" and "wasting their education."

In an atmosphere bristling with self-righteousness (on both sides), I wonder aloud if I am the only one troubled by the description of stay-at-home mothers as "not working." It is then that I am asked by one of the workers if I consider myself a feminist. I do, I say, and ask in return if she would like to know my definition of feminism. Heads nod, nobody looks at the clock. I say that I see feminism as one of the great liberation movements in human history. It is the movement to free democracy from patriarchy.

The room quiets. Light strains through windows on the outside wall. What had felt like a performance now gives way to a conversation that grips everyone's attention. I ask the women to notice how hot the emotional climate in the room became. I say what I say to my students: notice what happens when you substitute curiosity for judgment. And when I comment on the presumption of heterosexuality, tacit in the discussion so far, the outliers come in.

Perhaps because, in my version, feminism is not defined as an issue of women or of men, or as a battle between women and men, the women speak of the tensions they experience in their relationships not only with one another but also with men. What is fueling these divisions among women and the conflicts between women and men? When the allotted time ends, we are in the thick of it, and the attentive listening and respect, the curiosity that accompanies disagreement, along with

176

the surge of energy and hope, reflect a feminism now joined with its ethic of care.

I had approached the study of morality as a naturalist. As a graduate student in psychology, I had listened to the ways psychologists spoke about people and their lives. When I began my own research, I listened to how people speak of themselves and talk about others, the stories they tell about their lives. My ear was caught by the disparity between the voices of theory and the voices of people on the ground. The word "voice" was an obvious choice for capturing what I was hearing. Psychologists don't typically use the word "voice." But to me it seemed preferable to "self"—more precise, less abstract. Because voice is embodied and in language, it connects psychology with biology and culture without reducing it to either.

In conclusion, then, a feminist ethic of care is integral to the struggle to release democracy from the grip of patriarchy because it roots that struggle in the exigencies of survival, the evolutionary need to put children's well being first (ahead of concerns about women's chastity and the perpetuation and augmentation of male lineages). A feminist care ethic encourages the capacities that constitute our humanity and alerts us to the practices that put them at risk. I have used the word "patriarchy" to describe those attitudes and values, moral codes and institutions, that separate men from men as well as from women and divide women into the good and the bad. Coming from a psychological background, I have linked patriarchy with the fragmentation of the psyche and thus with trauma. As long as human qualities are divided into masculine and feminine, we will be alienated from one another and from ourselves. The aspirations we hold in common, for love and for freedom, will continue to elude us.

In our seminar on resisting injustice, David and I require our students to work collaboratively in writing and performing short plays. We find that these theater exercises enliven classroom discussion and encourage original work. In our final class in the fall of 2009, the last group of students put on their play, a contemporary version of the *Oresteia*. They called it "Oresta Palin," with Sarah Palin's family as the twenty-first century's house of Atreus. In the play, conceived as a reality show, "American Justice," on Fox TV, Sarah Hrdy, the evolutionary anthropologist, appears as a modern-day Cassandra, speaking the truth but not heard or believed by the Fox News anchor.

At the outset, I confessed to being optimistic, but I am not naïve. As a psychologist interested in development, my eye always seeks out the edge, the place where progress can occur, where walls can come tumbling down. In my students, I listen for the new voice, the insight or connection that takes me by surprise. In my own research, what surprised me most was the discovery of a voice I knew but had forgotten. And perhaps this is what continues to fuel my optimism: that we have within ourselves the potential to free our humanity from a false story. With the advances in the human sciences, it is not knowledge we lack. In the words of Lindqvist, the Swedish journalist, "What is missing is the courage to understand what we know and to draw conclusions." The grounds for resistance are in our midst.

In *The Zookeeper's Wife*, Diane Ackerman tells the story of Antonina Zabinska's life in Warsaw during the Nazi occupation. Antonina tried telling herself that the sad reality of the war with its losses and funereal silences "wasn't a death sleep but hibernation." Living with animals, she knew that

> the lull of bats and polar bears . . . was only a rest cure during the icequake and frostbite days of winter when food hid and it was better to sleep in one's burrow, warmed by a storehouse of summer fat . . . Hibernation time wasn't only for sleep, it was also when bears typically gave birth to cubs they suckled and nuzzled until spring, a time of ripeness. (p. 98)

During the frigid winter in occupied Warsaw, with spirits shriveled by fear and cold and deprivation, she wonders: could the war days be seen not as a death of the spirit but as "a sort of hibernation of the spirit, when ideas, knowledge, science, enthusiasm for work, understanding and love—all accumulate inside, [where] nobody can take them away from us" (p. 98). Meanwhile, she hid over 300 Jews in the zoo and dissuaded the Nazis who came to her door from searching the cages.

In June of 2010 in the Sorbonne's *Amphitheater Descartes*, the ethic of care emerged from a kind of hibernation. A conference on care ethics was held in this center of civilization. On the day of the conference, as the amphitheater fills, I savor the irony of coming to the *salon Descartes* to heal Cartesian splits. These splits have blunted our ethical intelligence, fragmented our psyches, short-circuited our neurology, compromised democracy, and jeopardized our survival. We register the loss in our bodies and our emotions, and our lives become tinged with trauma and tragedy. This is an old story, one we know. In the new story, the capacity for empathy, mind-reading, and collaboration distinguishes us not as women and men but as humans. Within ourselves we have the resources we need. However adverse the political climate, however bad the weather, they accumulate inside where nobody can take them away from us.

In nature, spring—the time of ripeness when hibernation ceases—happens only once a year. In the psyche, the potential is always present. The time to act is now.

Acknowledgments

My greatest debt is to my students who over the years have accompanied me on this journey, and to the women and men, girls and boys who participated in my research. Their voices inspired me, and I quote many of them in this book. A special thanks to Dana Edell, Matthew Graziano, and Chera Reid. I am also indebted to my colleagues: to David Richards from whom I have learned so much about ethical resistance and whose generosity moves me deeply, to Sandra Laugier and Patricia Papperman whose efforts on behalf of care ethics led to the revised French translation of *In a Different Voice*, to Elisabeth Young-Bruehl and Christine Dunbar for their generous and informative response to the chapter on psychoanalysis, and to Niobe Way, who put in place the final piece of a puzzle I had been working on since the time I first met her, many years ago, when she came to Harvard as a graduate student. She has become a best friend as well as a beloved colleague, and several ideas presented here were sparked or refined at our Wednesday breakfasts. But the book itself would not have come into being without the encouragement and friendship of John Thompson; for his intelligence and sensibility, I am most grateful.

My thanks as well to Terri Apter, Tova Hartman, Dana Crowley Jack, Robert Moeller, Wendy Puriefoy, Randy Testa, and Niobe Way for their responses to earlier drafts of the manuscript, to Betsy Lerner, my agent, who read when she didn't have to, to Emily Hass, my assistant, to Paul Lippmann, Marilyn Charles, Phillip Blumberg, and Henry Friedman for encouraging this project, to Rachel Kadish and Mark Blechner for their suggestions, to Tim Clark for his excellent copy-editing, to Carole Obedin for her wisdom, and to my grandchildren—Nora, Jacob, Maxine, Benjamin, Noah, and Joseph Gilligan—who keep alive my delight in children's perceptiveness and my faith in the future.

Tina Packer did what only the best of friends will do: read every single word of this book, bringing to it her finely tuned ear for language and her eye for the dramatic line. As I was writing *Joining the Resistance* she was writing *Women of Will*, based on the theater piece she created and performed, and along the way we reinforced in one another our sense of the need to tell a new story.

To Jim, my love, my companion in life, and the reader I count on, my thanks for everything, including your willingness to be part of this story.

Note on the text

The research that forms the backbone of this book was conducted over many years and in a variety of settings, starting with the studies that led to *In a Different Voice*. I have chosen a few examples from that book to illustrate certain points, and Judy and Anna, along with several other girls quoted briefly here, are discussed at greater length in *Meeting at the Crossroads*. An extended discussion of the research on young boys and their fathers, and of the different versions of Anne Frank's diary, can be found in Part II of *The Birth of Pleasure*.

I would like to thank Harvard University Press for permission to reprint the examples adapted from *In a Different Voice: Psychological Theory and Women's Development* (© 1982, 1993 by Carol Gilligan) and from *Meeting at the Crossroads* (portions of chapter 4 appeared in a different form on Meeting at the Crossroads: Women's Psychology and Girls' Development by Lyn Mikel Brown and Carol Gilligan, pp. 123–41, 185–95, Cambridge Mass.: Harvard University Press, Copyright © 1992 by the President and Fellows of Harvard College); Cambridge University Press for permission to reprint some material from *The Deepening Darkness: Patriarchy, Resistance and Democracy's Future* (© 2009 Carol Gilligan and David A. J. Richards), and the journal *Contemporary Psychoanalysis*, in which an earlier and substantially different version of Chapter 3 appeared. My thanks also to the University of Michigan Press for permission to include "Joining the Resistance," originally a lecture from 1990 "Joining the Resistance: Psychology, Politics, Girls and Women," by Carol Gilligan from *The Female Body*, edited by Laurence Goldstein (© 1991, The University of Michigan Press), now revised and expanded as Chapter 4 of this book, and to Princeton

University Press for permission to reprint parts of "The Age of Reason," from Jorie Graham's, *Erosion* (© Princeton University Press, 1983).

In revisiting and presenting my current take on my earlier work, I have selected those cases and examples that I find most telling. More detailed information about both the studies and the research participants can be found in the relevant works listed in the References.

References

Ackerman, Diane. *The Zookeeper's Wife: A War Story.* New York: W.W. Norton, 2007.

Adelson, Joseph. *Handbook of Adolescent Psychology.* New York: Wiley, 1980.

Aeschylus. *The Oresteia.* Translated and edited by David R. Slavitt. Philadelphia: University of Pennsylvania Press, 1998.

Apuleius. *Metamorphoses.* Edited and translated by J. Arthur Hanson. Cambridge, MA: Harvard University Press, Loeb Classical Library, 1989.

Aristophanes. *Lysistrata / The Acharnians / The Clouds.* Translated by Alan H. Sommerstein, London: Penguin Books, 1973.

BBC News. "The Christmas Truce." Special Report, October 1998 (Adapted from *Christmas Truce* by Malcolm Brown and Shirley Seaton).

Berger, John. *G. A Novel.* London: Bloomsbury, 1972.

Bernardez, Teresa. "Women and Anger: Cultural Prohibitions and The Feminine Ideal." Wellesley

College: Stone Center Working Paper Series, 31, 1988.

Blumenthal, Ralph. "Five Precious Pages Renew Wrangling over Anne Frank." *New York Times*, September 10, 1998.

Bornstein, David. "Fighting Bullying with Babies." *The New York Times Opinionator*, November 8, 2010.

Bowlby, John. *Loss: Sadness and Depression*. New York: Basic Books, 1980.

Breuer, Josef and Sigmund Freud. *Studies on Hysteria* (1895). *The Standard Edition of the Complete Psychological Works of Sigmund Freud*, Vol. II. Translated and edited by James Strachey. London: The Hogarth Press, 1955.

Brown, Lyn Mikel and Carol Gilligan. *Meeting at the Crossroads: Women's Psychology and Girls' Development*. Cambridge, MA: Harvard University Press, 1992.

Chu, Judy. "Learning What Boys Know." Ed.D Dissertation, Harvard University, 2000.

Coles, Robert. *Children of Crisis: A Study in Courage and Fear*. Boston: Atlantic-Little Brown, 1967.

Collins, Gail. *When Everything Changed: The Amazing Journey of American Women From 1960 to the Present*. New York: Little Brown, 2009.

Damasio, Antonio. *Descartes' Error: Emotion, Reason, and the Human Brain*. New York: Putnam Publishing Group, 1994.

—— *The Feeling of What Happens: Body and Emotion in the Making of Consciousness*. San Diego: Harcourt, 1999.

de Waal, Frans. *The Age of Empathy: Nature's Lessons*

for a Kinder Society. New York: Harmony Books, 2009.

Devereux, George. "Why Oedipus Killed Laius: A Note on the Complementary Oedipus Complex in Greek Drama." *International Journal of Psycho-Analysis*, 34, 1953: 132–41.

Dostoevsky, Fyodor. *The Brothers Karamazov*. Translated by Richard Pevear and Larissa Volokhonsky. New York: Farrar, Straus, and Giroux, 2002.

Elder, Glen and Avshalom Caspi. "Studying Lives in a Changing Society: Sociological and Personological Explorations." In A Rabin et al. (eds.), *Studying Persons and Lives*. New York: Springer, 1990.

Ferenczi, Sandor. "Confusion of Tongues Between Adults and Child: The Language of Tenderness and of Passion." In M. Balint (ed.), *Final Contributions to the Problems and Methods of Psycho-Analysis*. New York: Brunner/Mazel, 1980 (1955).

Frank, Anne. *The Diary of Anne Frank: The Critical Edition*. Prepared by the Netherlands State Institute for War Documentation. Edited by David Barnouw and Gerrold Van Der Stroom. Translated by Arnold J. Poermans and B. M. Mooyaart. New York: Doubleday, 1989.

Franklin, Nancy. "Teachers' Tales of Empowerment: A Story From an English Teacher." Paper presented at the Harvard-Laurel Conference on The Psychology of Women and The Education of Girls, April 6, 1990, Cleveland, Ohio.

Freud, Sigmund. *The Interpretation of Dreams* (1899/1900). *The Standard Edition of the Complete*

Psychological Works of Sigmund Freud, Vols IV and V. Translated and edited by James Strachey. London: The Hogarth Press, 1955.

—— "On the Universal Tendency to Debasement in the Sphere of Love" (1912). *Standard Edition*, Vol. XI, pp. 177–91.

—— *New Introductory Lectures on Psycho-Analysis* (1933). *Standard Edition*, Vol. XXII.

—— *The Complete Letters of Sigmund Freud to Wilhelm Fliess, 1887–1904*. Translated and edited by Jeffrey Moussaieff Masson. Cambridge, MA: Harvard University Press, 1985.

Gilligan, Carol. *In a Different Voice: Psychological Theory and Women's Development*. Cambridge, MA: Harvard University Press, 1982.

—— *The Birth of Pleasure*. New York: Alfred A. Knopf, 2002 (Vintage paperback edition: *The Birth of Pleasure: A New Map of Love*, 2003).

—— *Kyra: A Novel*. New York: Random House, 2008.

Gilligan, Carol and David A.J. Richards. *The Deepening Darkness: Patriarchy, Resistance, and Democracy's Future*. New York: Cambridge University Press, 2009.

Gilligan, Carol and Jonathan Gilligan. "The Scarlet Letter: A play inspired by Hawthorne's novel." Unpublished script, 2007.

Gilligan, Carol, Renee Spencer, Katherine Weingarten, and Tatiana Bertsch. "On the Listening Guide: A Voice-Centered, Relational Method." In Paul M. Camic, Jean E. Rhodes, and Lucy Yardley (eds.), *Qualitative Research in Psychology: Expanding Perspectives in Methodology and Design*. Washington,

D.C.: American Psychological Association Press, 2003.

Gogol, Nikolai. *The Overcoat and Other Tales of Good and Evil.* W.W. Norton, 1965 (1842).

Graham, Jorie. *Erosion.* Princeton, N.J.: Princeton University Press, 1983.

Grumet, Madeline. *Bitter Milk: Women and Teaching.* Amherst, MA: University of Massachusetts Press, 1988.

Hallie, Philip P. *Lest Innocent Blood be Shed: The Story of the Village of Le Chambon and How Goodness Happened There.* New York: Harper and Row, 1979.

Hawthorne, Nathaniel. *The Scarlet Letter.* New York: The Modern Library, 2000 (1850).

Herbert, Bob. "Women at Risk." *New York Times,* August 8, 2009.

Hrdy, Sarah Blaffer. *Mothers and Others: The Evolutionary Origins of Mutual Understanding.* Cambridge, MA: Harvard University Press, 2009.

King, Martin Luther Jr. "Letter from a Birmingham Jail." (1963) in *I Have a Dream: Writings and Speeches That Changed the World.* New York: HarperCollins, 1992.

Koonz, Claudia. *Mothers in the Fatherland: Women, the Family, and Nazi Politics.* New York: St. Martin's Press, 1987.

Kristoff, Nicholas D. and Sheryl WuDunn. *Half the Sky: Turning Oppression into Opportunity for Women Worldwide.* New York: Alfred A. Knopf, 2009.

Krull, Marianne. *Freud and His Father.* New York: W.W. Norton, 1986 (1979).

Laugier, Sandra. "Care et Perception: L'Ethique comme

attention au particulier." In P. Papperman and S. Laugier (eds.), *Le souci des autres: Ethiques et politiques du care*. Paris: Editions de L'EHESS collection *Raisons pratiques*, 2005. (English translation, *Care Ethics as Attention to Particulars*, forthcoming.)

LeDoux, Joseph. *The Emotional Brain*. New York: Simon and Schuster, 1996.

Levy, Ariel. "Lift and Separate: Why is Feminism Still so Divisive?" *The New Yorker*, November 16, 2009.

Lindqvist, Sven. *Exterminate All the Brutes: One Man's Odyssey into the Heart of Darkness and the Origins of European Genocide*. Translated by Joan Tate. New York: The New Press, 1996 (1992).

Lipman, Joanne. "The Mismeasure of Women." *New York Times*, October 24, 2009.

Mann, Sally. *Proud Flesh*. New York: Aperture/ Gagosian Gallery, 2009.

—— Artist's statement for exhibit "Proud Flesh." Gagosian Gallery, New York, N.Y., September 15– October 31, 2009.

Muller, Melissa. *Anne Frank: The Biography*. Translated by Robert Kimber and Rita Kimber. New York: Henry Holt & Co., 1998 (1996).

Nurock, Vanessa (ed.). *Carol Gilligan et l'ethique du care*. Paris: Presses Universitaires de France, 2010.

Packer, Tina. *Women of Will: Following the Feminine in Shakespeare's Plays*. New York: Alfred A. Knopf, forthcoming.

Papperman, Patricia. "Les gens vulnerables n'ont rien d'exceptionnel." In P. Papperman and S. Laugier (eds.), *Le souci des autres: Ethiques et politiques du care*. Paris: Éditions de L'EHESS collection *Raisons pratiques*, 2005. (English translation, *Care Ethics as Attention to Particulars*, forthcoming.)

Richards, David A.J. *Women, Gays, and the Constitution: The Grounds for Feminism and Gay Rights in Culture and Law*. Chicago: University of Chicago Press, 1998.

—— *Disarming Manhood: Roots of Ethical Resistance*. Athens, Ohio: Swallow Press, 2005.

Rilling, James K., David A. Gutman, Thorsten R. Zeh, Guiseppe Paqgnoni, Gregory S. Berns, Clinton D. Kilts. "A Neural Basis for Social Cooperation." *Neuron*, 35, 2, July 2002: 395–405.

Roy, Arundhati. *The God of Small Things*. New York: Harper Perennial, 1998.

Ruddick, Sara. *Maternal Thinking: Toward a Politics of Peace*. Boston: Beacon Press, 1989.

Rushdie, Salman. *Haroun and the Sea of Stories*. New York: Penguin Books, 1991 (1990).

Schorske, Carl. *Fin de Siècle Vienna: Politics and Culture*. New York: Vintage Books, 1981.

Sennett, Richard. *Together: The History, Rituals, Pleasures and Politics of Cooperation*. New Haven: Yale University Press, 2011.

Slote, Michael. A. *Essays on the History of Ethics*. New York: Oxford University Press, 2009.

—— "The Spectrum of Ethical Theories." Paper given at the University of Miami, September, 19, 2008.

Slovo, Shawn. *A World Apart*. London: Faber and Faber, 1988.

Suttie, Ian. D. *The Origins of Love and Hate*. London: Free Association, 1999 (1935).

Tatlow, Didi Kirsten. "Freudians Put China on the Couch." *New York Times* reprints, October 28, 2010.

Virgil. *The Aeneid.* Translated by H. Rushton Fairclough. Cambridge, MA: Harvard University Press, Loeb Classical Library, 1999.

Way, Niobe. *Deep Secrets: Boys' Friendships and the Crisis of Connection.* Cambridge, MA: Harvard University Press, 2011.

Williams, Tennessee. *A Streetcar Named Desire.* New York: New Directions, 2004 (1947).

Woolf, Virginia. *Three Guineas.* Jane Marcus edition. Orlando, FL: Harvest, 2006 (1938).

Young-Bruehl, Elisabeth. *Childism: Understanding and Preventing Prejudice Against Children.* New Haven: Yale University Press, forthcoming.

Young-Bruehl, Elisabeth and Christine Dunbar. Email communication, November 8, 2010.